GETCONNECTED

Mobilizing Your Church for God's Mission

GETCONNECTED

Mobilizing Your Church for God's Mission

JOHNNY M. HUNT
AND FRIENDS

Dewey Decimal Classification: 266.023
Subject Heading: FOREIGN MISSIONS

Profits will be used to help support more than 5,000 missionaries currently
serving around the world through IMB.

Scripture quotations are from the Holman Christian Standard Bible.
© 1999, 2000, 2002, 2003 by Holman Bible Publishers, Nashville,
Tennessee. All rights reserved.

"Defining Moment" lyric used by permission from Eddie Carswell. Song by
Moore, Buck; Ahlstrom, Leonard; Carswell, Eddie; © 2000 by Sony.

Lottie Moon Christmas Offering® and Annie Armstrong Easter Offering®
are registered trademarks of WMU®.

Editors: Erich Bridges, Nancy Robertson, and Anita Bowden,
    Richmond, Virginia
Cover and Interior Design: Susan Browne Design, Nashville, Tennessee

Printed in the United States of America
1 2 3 4 5 6 7 8 9 10   15 14 13 12 11 10

CONTENTS

Johnny Hunt, atop
Mount Nebo, looks
across the Holy Land.

FOREWORD

JERRY RANKIN

I had the privilege to preach at First Baptist Church of Woodstock, Ga., during a recent Global Impact Celebration. The fervent worship of more than 7,500 members and visitors reflected a passion for God and His glory among the nations. At least 50 missionary partners were introduced from around the world. They had shared in Sunday School classes, home fellowships, and church-wide events throughout the week. In the Sunday morning worship service, 139 short-term volunteers were commissioned who would be leaving for missions trips later in the month to four countries overseas. They represented only a portion of the more than 1,000 Woodstock members who are involved in mission trips throughout North America and around the world each year. At the end of the service, the congregation was challenged to pledge more than $4 million to the missions budget beyond normal tithes and church gifts!

I will never forget the first time I met Pastor Johnny Hunt. I had recently been elected president of IMB and was speaking to a group of pastors in the Atlanta area. Several reported on recent mission trips and what their churches were doing in missions support. Pastor Johnny addressed the group and asked, "How many of you promote giving to the Lottie Moon Christmas Offering for International Missions® by saying, 'Everyone cannot go, but everyone can give'?" Most of the pastors raised their hands. He responded with passion, "That's a lie! Everyone can go, and you'll never have a mission-minded church until you provide opportunities and challenge them to go. Only then will they give generously and sacrificially."

Pastor Johnny then described how missions had become the passion of his ministry and the priority of his church. He declared that getting people involved in mission trips was the primary factor in the growth Woodstock had experienced. He explained that when people go overseas, or to an unchurched area of the United States, they are confronted with lostness, they see God at work, and they realize they ought to do at home what they went on a mission trip to do.

I speak in churches across the Southern Baptist Convention practically every Sunday. It is not unusual to have lunch with the pastor after Sunday morning worship and for him to say something like: "Dr. Rankin, we appreciate your coming to present a mission challenge to our church. We are trying to build up our programs, reach our community, and pay off our indebtedness. Then we are going to get our people involved in missions."

However, that seldom happens. A church that ignores the Great Commission to focus only on local ministry becomes self-centered and ingrown. Seldom do such churches fulfill the criteria they have set to move to the next level and become engaged in missions. Missions is not an either/or proposition, yet many pastors are depriving their churches of the very thing that would stimulate spiritual vitality and growth—involvement in missions.

Then there are churches that keep missions before their people, lead them to adopt and pray for unreached people groups, challenge them to give generously and sacrificially to missions, provide opportunities for short-term trips, and call out members to give their lives to missionary service. I have yet to see a congregation fitting that description that is not growing in local outreach and ministry. This book contains the testimonies of several such churches. But it doesn't happen until the pastor catches the vision, and a passion for missions becomes the driving force of his ministry. As Pastor Johnny often says, "The light that shines the farthest shines the brightest at home."

A theme throughout my tenure of leadership has been that it is not the responsibility of IMB to do missions on behalf of Southern Baptists. The Great Commission was given to every believer and to every church. The responsibility of IMB as the mission agency of the SBC is to mobilize, facilitate, and enable every church to be obedient to the Great Commission!

We will never have enough missionaries to reach a lost world. However, God has raised up Southern Baptists in numbers and resources, not to take pride in being a great denomination, but to be His instrument to reach a lost world. If 45,000 churches with 16 million members catch a vision for what they can do and become strategically involved, the whole world will be reached with the Gospel.

If you think only mega-churches such as FBC Woodstock have the capacity for strategic involvement in missions, this book will give you a glimpse into the hearts of a variety of pastors who have led their churches into exciting mission partnerships around the world. Some of their churches are small (like Woodstock was when it got started in missions), yet they have dared to believe God and courageously respond to the vision of discipling the nations. Not only have they had the joy of seeing lost people around the world changed by their witness, their churches have grown as their members experience a new dimension of serving God.

You will be challenged and encouraged by Pastor Johnny Hunt and his friends as you read about how their churches got connected on mission with God!

Chapter One

LET GOD CAPTURE YOUR HEART

JOHNNY M. HUNT

Senior Pastor, First Baptist Church, Woodstock, Ga.

I'm a pastor. Whatever else I may do in life, that's what God called me to *be*.

I love encouraging other pastors. Here's my message in 10 words: You teach what you know; you reproduce who you *are*.

You can preach all you want about reaching the world for Christ, but if you don't get out there on the edge with your people, they won't go.

I'm 57. During the last 20-plus years, God has given me the opportunity to lead First Baptist Woodstock—a church that was struggling to survive in the 1980s—to a position of global influence. More than 7,000 people worship with us each week. We baptized nearly 700 people in 2009. We've planted more than 80 churches around the United States. Every year we send hundreds of volunteers to share Jesus Christ and train leaders all over the world. We partner strategically with missionaries to take the Gospel to unreached peoples in some of the darkest places on earth. We support more than 100 missionary families in our nation and overseas.

It's an exciting place to be. But I never forget where I came from: Nesby Courts, a government-subsidized housing project in Wilmington, N.C. My dad was a hard worker, but he left my mother, my five siblings, and me when I was 7 years old. That hurt, and it gave me an excuse to get into trouble. I started getting drunk at age 11. I dropped out of high school (I wasn't a bad student, but I skipped more classes than I attended), raced my Pontiac GTO at the local drag strip, and hung out at the Sunset Park Poolroom, which I later managed.

I knew how to play some pool, brother, and I knew how to swing my fists—or my pool cue—if things got out of hand.

The Lord Jesus saved me out of that life when I was 20—and called me into His service. And because He so loves the world, He told me to go back down to the Sunset Park Poolroom and tell my rowdy buddies what He had done for me. I was so excited, I told anybody who would listen. I didn't even know the right Bible verses to lead someone to Jesus. I just knew He had changed me forever, and I wanted the world to know it!

Do you know who first invited me to church (besides my patient wife, Janet, who put up with a lot in those days) and taught me how to share Jesus with others? Two laymen.

N.W. Pridgen used to come into the hardware store where I worked. He would ask me, week after week, to visit Long Leaf Baptist Church in Wilmington, where I eventually gave my heart to Christ. After finishing college and seminary, I came back to be pastor of that little church. I'm not sure what N.W. saw in me, but he was faithful to God in reaching out to a troubled young man.

The other layman was Alfred Joyner, a truck driver. He taught me how to share the Gospel by taking me with him to visit lost folks. With Alfred, it was just a natural thing. I'd been saved maybe two or three weeks. Alfred said, "Now that you've gotten saved, we need to get you out witnessing." He'd take me to the home of some rough customer from the pool hall, since he had been converted out of that type of life, too. I thought he would do all the talking, but right in the middle of the visit, Alfred would say, "Johnny, tell about what Jesus did for you."

> I didn't even know what "discipling" or "mentoring" meant in those days, but Alfred was discipling and mentoring me.

He showed me the verses about sin and salvation in the little "Soul Winner's" New Testament the church gave me. We visited homes a few times, and then one day Alfred said, "I can't make it tonight, Johnny, but you go ahead without me." I was nervous, but I went, and I found out what God can do through anyone who makes himself available. I didn't even know what "discipling" or "mentoring" meant in those days, but Alfred was discipling and mentoring me. We're still friends to this day. After 37-plus years, look at the impact this man made in my life.

I want to do that for others!

MISJUDGING OUR CAPACITY FOR GOD

I mention my early days—and these two faithful laymen—for a reason. The great preacher and evangelist C.H. Spurgeon made a statement that challenges me and should challenge you: "We have misjudged our capacity for God." A lot of pastors are selling themselves and their people short when it comes to how much God can accomplish through them. We need to realize how great God is. It's not what we bring to Him; it's what He brings to us and does through us—*if* we give Him a chance to work.

Who would have believed that God could reach into a government project, grab a high school dropout (me), and allow him to pastor one of the significant churches in the country? Or to serve as president of the Southern Baptist Convention, the largest Protestant denomination in the United States? We've misjudged our capacity for God. If young pastors will begin to dream—and older pastors will begin to dream again—God will use us. Janet and I pray constantly that God will use us significantly each day.

I hear many pastors say, "Well, I'm just a country preacher," or "We're a small church. We can't do that much." That's not an indictment of them; it's an indictment against the God who lives in them. No one, and no church, is insignificant—regardless of where you are. With Christ,

> If young pastors will begin to dream—
> and older pastors will begin to dream again—
> God will use us.

you can be not only significant but history-changing. I've often said that the New Testament shouts *position* in Christ over *location* in the world. Paul would say, "Paul, an apostle of Jesus Christ ..." wherever he was as he wrote, even if he sat in a Roman jail cell. Where he was in Christ was far more significant than where he was in the world.

Sometimes pastors think, "If I could just be in Atlanta ..." or, "If I were in Dallas ... ." No. Wherever you are, you can be significant there—globally significant. Who would have dreamed that a middle-aged preacher, starting over after many years out of the ministry, could lead a little country church in South Carolina to play a vital, historic

In the Middle East and North Africa, I saw once again how hungry people are for the truth of the Gospel. When they hear of the resurrected life of Christ, they are overwhelmed. They wonder why we waited so long to tell them!

role in reaching Muslims in West Africa with the Gospel? Read all about it in *God Story* (Chapter 5, starting on p. 65).

People are seriously underchallenged in churches today. "There's gold in them thar pews," I like to say. I get to dig every week in a gold mine, and so do you as a pastor or church leader. Do you know the potential of your people? I'm finding out new things about people at Woodstock every day. I could give you hundreds of examples. Here's one: Recently I needed someone to help with some artwork for the church, so I made a statement from the pulpit. A guy came up afterward and said, "I'm one of the chief artists with Coca-Cola. I'd be glad to help you." He was sitting out there in the pews, and I had no idea.

You never know for sure who is out there or what their gifts are. You'll never find out unless you ask. Encourage them to do something. Believe in your people, cast a vision, and see what happens!

Too many pastors are giving too little of themselves for the cause of the Gospel. A great cause calls for a great commitment. Look at your most committed lay people. They have jobs and kids, yet look at what they give. How could I ever consider being a 40-hour man when I have folks who work a job 40 and 50 hours a week and then give the Lord 20 hours in ministry? I'm not a workaholic; I'm just excited about what God is doing among our people.

I tell pastors: One of the reasons you get discouraged is because you're measuring only what happens on Sunday. It's hard to get discouraged when you hear from your people through the week about life-changing ministry they're doing in the community. Or when you hear from other churches you started. Or when you hear from missionaries you partner with around the world. It's what I get up for in the morning. It's what I go to bed for at night, because I can't wait to get up tomorrow and get back to the church.

That's not just what I preach at Woodstock. It's in our DNA. Cut us and we bleed it.

Not only have we misjudged our capacity for God, we have misjudged what God wants to do. He wants the nations to worship Him. He is up to so much more than we know about, and He wants to do great things through us if we will be available to make His name great.

Psalm 67:1-4, one of the great mission passages of the Bible, says, "May God be gracious to us and bless us; look on us with favor so that Your way may be known on earth, Your salvation among all nations. Let the peoples praise You, God; let all the peoples praise You. Let the nations rejoice and shout for joy, for You judge the peoples with fairness and lead the nations on earth."

That is the purpose of the church. That is the purpose of missions. Pastor/writer John Piper said it so well:

"Missions is not the ultimate goal of the church. Worship is. Missions exists because worship doesn't. Worship is ultimate, not missions, because God is ultimate, not man. When this age is over, and the countless millions of the redeemed fall on their faces before the throne of God, missions will be no more. It is a temporary necessity. But worship abides forever."*

On that glorious day when missions is "no more," John the Apostle gives us a glimpse of what eternal worship will look like:

"After this I looked, and there was a vast multitude from every nation, tribe, people, and language, which no one could number, standing before the throne and before the Lamb. They were robed in white with palm branches in their hands. And they cried out in a loud voice: Salvation belongs to our God, who is seated on the throne, and to the Lamb! ..." (Revelation 7:9-10)

That is a vision worth sharing. You need to get God's heart for the world. When you do, it will change your whole ministry perspective.

You need to get connected!

NEW GENERATION, NEW CHURCH

Connecting to God's heart is our most urgent need, but it isn't our only one. We need to connect with our own church people. Especially young people. While we were sleeping, society changed. Our denomination changed. It's not in the process of changing; it *has* changed. So has every other church body in America.

I'm a baby boomer, but I'm close to the Builders generation that did so much to fund the modern evangelical mission movement after World War II. Their mentality was to give their money, send missionaries, and pray for 'em. The boomers kept giving and praying, but started going as mission volunteers. Today the Millennials (born

> While we were sleeping, society changed. Our denomination changed. It's not in the process of changing; it *has* changed.

after 1980) are moving into church leadership, and they want to *do* missions. Otherwise they won't get involved at all. They are saying, "We will give sacrificially, but we *must* go." It's not an option for them.

It's easier to get people to give their money than it is to get them to pray. It's easier to get people to give their money than it is to get them to go on mission. But if I can get someone to go, I get everything. Often we ask for people's resources, but the greatest resource of the church sits in its pew. It's not what they carry in their pockets, it's who they are.

Don't promote a "program." The younger generation doesn't even like the word "program." Frankly, it sickens them. I'm not talking about whether I agree or disagree with them. I'm telling you where they are. Show your people the vision of what you want to do. People follow a vision. Dollars follow people. We took in $350,000 my first year at Woodstock. We took in $19 million in 2009. But personal involvement comes first. I show people God's vision and the needs around the world, and I give them ways to get involved. When they take ownership, it's theirs. I have a hard time keeping up with them!

Here's a paradox: The younger people in our churches reflect American society as a whole in that they are the least committed we've ever known—until they get committed. When they get committed, they are the most committed! They are the ones who will say to you, "What's the toughest mission assignment you've got?" If we're going to Tibet in the winter, I might warn them that hardly anyone comes back without frostbite. They respond, "Sign me up." They want the challenge and thrill. They are the generation jumping off mountaintops on a kite. They like the acceleration, the exhilaration that comes from the hardest assignments.

Here's a paradox: The younger people in our churches reflect American society as a whole in that they are the least committed we've ever known— until they get committed.

They're also willing to sacrifice. We have five missionary families now in a tough area of Southeast Asia. One of the wives recently gave birth to her first child. She and her husband live in a house the size of the shed where I keep my lawnmower. They have gladly sacrificed the American dream for a much greater dream.

Man, they inspire me! They remind me of Lottie Moon, Southern Baptists' most famous missionary. Lottie Moon gave up the American dream. She gave up wealth, comfort, and anything else that could hijack her calling to go to China and share Jesus. Near the end of her long service there, when other missionaries were leaving because of war and hunger and turmoil, she basically said, "I can't leave my Chinese brothers and sisters. I have become one of them and one with them." She gave them her food. When she died of malnutrition on a ship in the harbor of Kobe, Japan, on Christmas Eve 1912, everything she owned was in one small box. Yet she changed history in her own lifetime. And God has captured our hearts for missions through her story ever since.

Like Lottie, we're going to have to sacrifice our passion for the American dream to accomplish our part in spreading the Gospel. We're doing a lot of good things, but are we doing the best things? When we stand before Christ, will we have taken what He gave us and used it in the regions where it was most needed? When you're not just taking a trip but you're really catching His heart for the nations, you'll give like never before—of your time, your treasure, and yourself.

In Lottie's day, only a few could go physically. We're in a very different day. We discovered recently that 83 percent of the new missionaries appointed by IMB in a commissioning service had been involved in previous volunteer or short-term service. Eighty-three percent! Now they're going back to the country or people group they served, or maybe to a different country. The more we involve our people, the more they're going to take personal ownership of the field that needs to be harvested. And people pay for what they own.

We need to provide people with more ways to get in—to our churches and our denomination.

At Woodstock, you may come to church because of the youth ministry on Wednesday night. You may come because of our children's ministry on Wednesday night. You may come through our "Timothy" ministry that teaches homeschoolers. You may come through our sports—soccer or Upward Basketball. You may come through our music ministry or school of music. You may come through our worship. You may come through a Sunday School class. Those are all roads that lead to First Baptist Woodstock.

Could there be more than one door into SBC missions? We've become too narrow in our approach to involving people. We've got the best mission support system in the world. But my allegiance is not to the system that supports the mission. My allegiance is to the mission: the Great Commission that Christ has given us. The door to a church's or a pastor's involvement may be the Cooperative Program. It may be a mission trip. It may be the Lottie Moon Christmas Offering for International Missions®. It may be personally underwriting a missionary. It may be getting involved in a strategic missionary partnership, where you start going to a country and working with the missionaries there to reach the lost. It may be "all of the above." But we shouldn't penalize folks for entering through different doors.

Yes, our churches have changed. Our denomination has changed. We need to acknowledge that and accommodate it, or we're going to lose a generation of men and women who want to serve God. Southern Baptists and other evangelicals must realize: If we don't develop the generation coming behind us, we don't have a future.

AWAKEN, EXPLORE, EQUIP, ENGAGE, MULTIPLY

At Woodstock, we've been partnering for more than 20 years with IMB and other Great Commission groups to reach the nations for Christ. IMB is working harder than ever to serve local churches and help us fulfill our mission to make disciples among all peoples. Make no mistake: It is *our* mission, not IMB's mission, or some parachurch agency's mission, or the mission of someone called to be a career missionary. It is the mission of the local church if we take Jesus at His word.

Jesus gave the Great Commission to *all* of His followers, not just to a group of professional missionaries, when He said, "Go, therefore, and make disciples of all nations, baptizing them in the name of the Father and of the Son and of the Holy Spirit" (Matthew 28:19). He was speaking to *all* of His followers when He said, "But you will receive

> If you see missions as just another menu item in the great cafeteria of church programs, you have made the Great Commission an option. It is not an option; it is the mission of the church!

power when the Holy Spirit has come upon you, and you will be My witnesses in Jerusalem, in all Judea and Samaria, and to the ends of the earth" (Acts 1:8).

Looking over the ruins of an ancient Byzantine church in the Middle East, I thought about how the mission of the church—the Great Commission—must be renewed in each generation. If we don't mobilize the generation coming behind us, we don't have a future.

If you see missions as just another menu item in the great cafeteria of church programs, you have made the Great Commission an option. It is not an option; it is the mission of the church! It starts at home (Jerusalem), but it goes to the ends of the earth. We need to teach our people what the Bible says about Jerusalem, Judea, Samaria, and the ends of the earth. But we need God's heart when we teach, not a selfish or narrow spirit that seeks to hoard our gifts and keep them close to home.

You don't need me to tell you how spiritually lost our country is today. Mission researchers tell us there are more lost people in America than any other nation besides China and India. But America has enjoyed freedom of religion and the free proclamation of the Gospel of Christ for most of its history.

Consider my state. Georgia has 9.7 million people. More than half of them live in metro Atlanta, which is Woodstock's greater "Jerusalem." That's a lot of folks. Yet there are more than 3,600 Southern Baptist churches in Georgia, not to mention all the other evangelical churches and forms of witnesses we have. But in the global areas of deepest lostness, there are about 1.6 billion people who have never even heard the name of Jesus. Unless we take what God has given us and make it available to these people, they will perish without the Gospel.

Are there more lost people in your area than you can reach? That will always be true, but it doesn't nullify the Great Commission. We're to be involved in the nations, regardless of the amount of work we have to do where we are. Even though Woodstock is a large church, we're not that large compared to the number of unchurched people in our area—millions in greater Atlanta, hundreds of thousands in our immediate community. Some church people will respond to the call to local ministry. Others will respond to the call to the nations. But we must issue the call—and let God work in their hearts. It's not either/or. It's both/and.

We need to mobilize the church in America to go to the unreached. Help your people realize the vastness of the lostness. Help them realize that 95 percent of the world's population lives outside of America. IMB mission researchers tell us there are more than 12,000 distinct people groups in the world ("the nations" as the Bible speaks of them). Nearly 6,500 of those groups are considered unreached, meaning fewer than 2 percent of their members are evangelical believers in Jesus Christ. These unreached people groups represent 1.6 billion people—25 percent of the world's population.

Many of these people have no access to the Gospel whatsoever—no known church, missionary or even a plan to reach them. These people groups are the "unengaged," and there are still nearly 3,500 of them in the world. If we don't go to them, who will?

Our partners at IMB use five simple verbs when they "coach" pastors and churches interested in connecting with the world: *awaken, explore, equip, engage, multiply.*

Chapter 6, *Make the Connection!* (p. 85), will give you a detailed, practical guide to all five steps in the connection journey. Here they are in a nutshell:

Awaken to God's heart that all people may know and worship Him.

Explore God's specific plan for your church.

Equip your church to fulfill the mission.

Engage in God's specific plan for your church.

Multiply your lives, mission, and ministry into other believers.

Every church is different in the way it responds to God's movement. I can't tell you how things will unfold at your church, but I can tell you a little of Woodstock's story. I also want to introduce you to four brother pastors God has given me the privilege of knowing and influencing:

Paul Purvis, pastor of First Baptist Church, Forsyth, Mo., came to our "Timothy+Barnabas" conference for pastors when he was serving at a church about an hour from Woodstock. He heard me talk about what we were doing in missions, and there came a time when I said, "Hey, I'd like for you to be involved. How about going on this overseas trip with me?" Now he's fully engaged in multiple places around the world. Read his story, *It's Not About Me*, starting on p. 31.

Richard Mark Lee, pastor of Sugar Hill (Ga.) Church, is a young guy who contacted me when he started ministry in the greater Atlanta area. I connected him with our mission work in Argentina, and he later branched out to Brazil. After going with me to the Middle East, where he has taken volunteer teams in the past, he's planning to lead his church to partner with IMB missionaries to reach the lost there. Richard is one of those leaders of the younger generation who is looking for direct, hands-on mission opportunities. He might not have connected to missions through our traditional denominational channels. But now that he's seen what God is doing, he's excited about mobilizing his church in strategic partnerships. Check out his journey, *Our Neighbors, the Nations, the Next Generation*, on p. 43.

Tim Anderson, pastor of Clements Baptist Church in Athens, Ala., was doing a great job leading his church in local ministry and evangelism. But he realized Clements wasn't fully obeying Christ's Acts 1:8 command as long they weren't going beyond their "Jerusalem" to the ends of the earth. So I invited him to go with me. Now they're working in Ukraine, Argentina, South Africa, and other places. His story, *Defining Moments*, starts on p. 53.

Brad Bessent, pastor of Beulah Baptist Church, Hopkins, S.C., is that middle-aged preacher I mentioned earlier, who started over in ministry after some difficult "wilderness" years. He came to spend some time with me and asked, "Will God ever use me again?" I was able to tell him, "God's not through with you. He's going to give you another opportunity." And He did. Beulah may be a small church, but God has given them a bigger opportunity to touch the world than Brad ever dreamed of! See *God Story* on p. 65.

START RELATIONALLY

You're probably detecting a method to my madness. It's pretty simple: When I go somewhere, I take somebody with me—just like Alfred Joyner took me witnessing with him when I was a new Christian.

I try to create platforms where pastors and church leaders can go and see the countless opportunities for them to get personally involved, to take ownership of missions. We've probably taken more than 100 pastors to the nations in the last 10 years. Some come from mega-churches like Woodstock; some come from small and medium-sized congregations. Once they get connected, they start inviting pastors to go with them, and the circle widens.

God has given me a ministry of mentoring pastors. Back in the late 1980s when Woodstock began to grow, I was speaking at various conferences and networking with a lot of people. Pastors began to call and say, "We'd like to come and spend a day with you," or "I need an hour on the phone," or "Could I take you to lunch?" I began to realize it was more than I could accommodate. So we started three-day gatherings where pastors could come, bring their wives, and we could just sit around and spend time together modeling ministry and mentoring. I try to instruct them as Paul instructed Timothy but also encourage them as Barnabas encouraged Paul. So God gave me the ministry of "Timothy+Barnabas"; I've been doing it for nearly 20 years now.

We do hours and hours of questions and answers. When there's a break, I'm there with them. I eat with them—breakfast, lunch, dinner. I'm never in a room by myself. I'm always with them. For three solid days, I pour myself into them. A lot of these guys come from small churches and don't have the budget to pay for the conference, so we often supplement or fully fund them. And we give them a lot of resources while they're with us. Last year we drew more than 1,400 leaders from 33 states.

Through Timothy+Barnabas International, we mentor hundreds of pastors in South America and other parts of the world, mobilizing them to go to the nations. The Great Commission is not just our mission. It belongs to the church universal. God is raising missionaries from all the mission fields! In fact, they are quickly surpassing us—the traditional missionary senders of the European and American churches—in their zeal for the task.

My basic point is this: You've got to make a personal connection in missions, just as you do in your day-to-day church ministry. You

The Muslim world is not unreachable. It is reachable. We need to make Christ known! Why is Woodstock able to make a real impact among these God-starved people? Because we have strategic mission partners through IMB who help us get in, get connected, and get going.

need to be relational. You don't build an effective team by making announcements from the pulpit, but through relationships around the table and in homes and in places of ministry and service with your people. You're equipping your people to do the work of the ministry.

A good pastor, like a good missionary, is working himself out of a job. An effective missionary reaches his people group with the Gospel, wins some to Christ, equips them, and turns the ministry over to them. The same pattern applies in the local church. If we don't develop our people to do the ministry, we're not doing biblical ministry. But you can develop your people only by pouring yourself into relationships.

I got started in international missions through a relationship.

Many years ago I told our folks I was praying God would give First Baptist Woodstock a ministry upon which the sun never sets. When we were sleeping, we'd have missionaries working in Indonesia, in Malaysia, in Thailand, all over the world. That was my dream, and it eventually came true. We have 120 families from Woodstock on the field. They go through IMB and other avenues, but they're sent from our church.

When I first voiced that dream, however, Woodstock was 150 years old and had never produced a missionary. But we had a former staff

> I had never been on an international mission trip. I knew nothing about Africa. Talk about being world-illiterate! When somebody would say "Kenya," I would ask, "Is that a city?"

member, Bruce Schmidt, who had become a missionary to Kenya with IMB. So I called Bruce in 1988 and asked, "How can we serve you?"

Bruce got excited. "The response to the Gospel here is unbelievable!" he said. "It's like an awakening. Everybody's getting saved. We can't get to 'em all. Bring a volunteer team. Let's do evangelism!"

I had never been on an international mission trip. I knew nothing about Africa. Talk about being world-illiterate! When somebody would say "Kenya," I would ask, "Is that a city?" I didn't know how to say Nairobi, Kenya, Africa. I didn't know how to separate the city from the country from the continent. I just knew Bruce was there, and he was a long way out in the bush. It was a scary endeavor, but I announced to the church we were going to be taking a trip. I think we took about 15 in the first group, and we went for 18 days.

We did evangelism in villages, evangelism in Nairobi, and training of pastors. A Holy Spirit revival was in full swing. From Nairobi to Mombasa on the north coast, Muslims were coming to Christ by the tens of thousands. Whole cities were being evangelized. One afternoon we baptized 5,000 new believers. Everywhere we went people wanted our Gospel tracts. And this was among a people group that had been resistant to the Gospel before things broke loose. God was up to something. The missionaries had planted and plowed and watered, and we were reaping where they had sown.

While we were there, I called back to Woodstock during a Sunday morning service. It was 3 a.m. in Kenya. I became extremely emotional as I tried to tell our folks what was happening, and I began to weep. Our associate pastor, who was on the other end of the telephone line, said, "Pastor, you need to know that while you're talking, the altars are flooded." God had come upon that place, and people came to the altars in tears.

That was it. God captured our hearts for the world. And He used a relationship with a missionary to do it. We were off and running. As we went to different parts of the world over the following years, we began to realize the need is great everywhere. The soil may not be as fertile, the people may not be as responsive, but the need always is great, and the lostness is deep.

START STRATEGICALLY

The deepest area of lostness, we know now, is among the unreached and unengaged peoples I talked about before—especially in the "10/40 Window," that huge band of the globe located between 10 and 40 degrees north of the equator stretching all the way from North Africa through Southeast Asia. That's where most of the major unreached peoples are located because of religious, cultural, and political barriers to the Gospel. And that's where a relationship—a *strategic* relationship— is even more important if we're to do missions effectively.

The local church is waking up to its role in the Great Commission, but that doesn't mean we don't need God-called, culturally trained, long-term missionaries who passionately love and deeply understand the people groups they are assigned to. I needed Bruce Schmidt to get us started in missions. We need missionary partners even more to get anywhere in the "10/40."

I see a lot of churches led by enthusiastic young pastors who ride off to the mission field with no vision, no strategic relationship, no plan. They "fire a shot" here and there and come home with some great stories, but it often ends there. Don't try to be Indiana Jones, the solo hero who barely makes it back alive. Be a team player, a coach, and a mobilizer. Cast a vision. Invite people to go with you. Work with a knowledgeable mission partner who knows his field. You'll make a much more lasting impact.

Recently Woodstock came full circle in our outreach to one major people group in the 10/40 world. We helped pioneer "Northern Lights," a longstanding IMB partnership project that uses volunteers every year to share Gospel materials with North African Muslim families who pass through seaports on the European side of the Mediterranean for vacation or business. It wasn't possible to connect with them in their own countries, but we could give them Bibles and *JESUS* films as they boarded ships and ferries in southern Europe to go home.

We sent teenagers at first, but the Northern Africans did not receive them well because they respect white hair and the wisdom it represents. So we started sending senior adults, who were treated with respect. The Muslim families would gladly receive a copy of God's Word from them, and it was a great impetus in our mission ministry to get senior adults involved in front-line missions.

Last year I went to the Middle East and North Africa with some fellow pastors and IMB partners, and I had the privilege of seeing with my own eyes the lands where we've been sending the Gospel through the "Northern Lights" project. One of the Northern African countries I visited is home to some of the most radical Islamic groups in the world. But it also is home to a powerful, indigenous church-planting movement that is expanding rapidly despite violent resistance.

Some of the new church leaders in the region are themselves former Muslim extremists. We listened to their stories. We met men who have known the Lord maybe five years, who sense the call to go back to their

> One pastor I met said the government had
> warned him to close his church. He refused.
> "What if they come back and arrest you?" I asked.
> "If that happens, God wants me to evangelize
> the prisons," he declared.

own people or their own villages, which are areas of hostility. They're willing to cross any barrier to make Christ known. They're averaging 450 to 500 people in their churches, and they're doing door-to-door evangelism at incredible risk. They are leading so many people to Christ that some Muslim evangelists in the region now copy their methods!

Live or die, there's no turning back for these church leaders. One pastor I met said the government had warned him to close his church. He refused. "What if they come back and arrest you?" I asked.

"If that happens, God wants me to evangelize the prisons," he declared.

We're not talking about the church in hiding. We're talking about bold proclaimers of the Good News. It reminds me of the book of Acts. How can we help these courageous believers? They need our prayer support—and they need the Old Testament in their language (a New Testament translation is available). There's a great hunger among people who have never owned their own Bible. We'll be partnering with IMB workers in the region any way we can.

People who have converted out of Islam in these areas tell us it's not that they didn't want to know about Jesus, it's that there was no one to tell them. When they hear of the resurrected life of Christ, of the joy and power He gives, they're overwhelmed. They wonder why we waited so long to tell them! They're really waiting. There's far more openness among the common people than we've ever known. We have concentrated too much on radical Islam when the truth is that most of it is nominal at best. We have to get out of our mindset that the Muslim world is not reachable. It is reachable. Christ needs to be made known!

And why is Woodstock able to make a real impact among these God-starved people? Because we have strategic mission partners through IMB who help us get in, get connected, and get going.

There's no shortage of resources to help you get connected. The last chapter of this book, *Make the Connection!*, is a very practical guide IMB uses to "coach" pastors and churches on how to get started. At Woodstock, we've written a training manual called *Strategic Missionary Partnerships* that's being used by churches across the United States.

Our approach is not just to show up somewhere and hope for the best. We say: Let's come up with a plan. Let's lay it out. Let's work with missionaries. Let's ask them, "What do you want us to do, and where can we be five years from now if we're strategic?" How can we bring missionaries to our church when they're in the United States to stay with us and train us? We want them here so our folks can meet them. We want to say to them, "Tell us what you need and how we can serve you." Then we'll build a team to go and serve their need. We'll serve them, not the other way around. The goal is to reach the lost, not to serve our own needs.

Another excellent ministry called Global Focus (globalfocus.info) has joined hands with IMB to help churches see the big picture and get connected. They do a great job of going into churches and teaching them how to connect with missionaries and strategic mission partners.

START SMALL

I hear this statement all the time: "You're big at Woodstock. You've got the resources to do anything you want." Well, we were doing missions at Woodstock long before we reached the size we are today. We may be able to undertake big projects now, but in earlier days we took a *piece of one project*. Smaller groups within our church still do.

If you want an example of how God can use a small group to do great things in missions, consider one of our Sunday School classes. It's led by a dynamic young man who is a banker in our community. Here is his testimony:

When I joined Woodstock, I didn't get involved in leadership initially, probably for a lot of the wrong reasons. I was "taking a break." That's one of the challenges in a church our size. It's easy to come here on Sunday morning and feel good about all the ministry you are associated with—as opposed to actually being engaged in.

Well, they challenged me to get off my backside and get involved. It comes from Pastor all the way down. It's hard to be around this ministry, if you are truly walking with the Lord, and not be stirred to find out what you can do. I've been teaching for about four years. In our Sunday School class, we're trying to relate to all four parts of Acts 1:8—Jerusalem, Judea, Samaria, and the uttermost parts. We've got something in each bucket: local, regional, national, and international. Internationally, we're going to one of the most challenging countries of Central Asia. Coordinating Woodstock's outreach to that nation is a function of our class.

We average between 20 and 30 people in our class on a Sunday morning. God has just burdened our hearts with the people of that land. That's a result of going over there, meeting the people, and engaging them with the Gospel. Now our primary goal is organizing the work not just for our Sunday School class but to the extent that it involves the rest of the church. How are we going to strategically, intentionally, and practically go about ministering to that nation?

Is that cool or what? He will call me sometimes for advice. He'll apologize for calling since I'm so "busy," to which I respond, "You are the epitome of a pastor's dream! Call me anytime!" Where we were supporting him to go at first, now he's supporting us. He's taken over the mission. That's how you make a disciple. Now he can do it without me. He can lead a team into Central Asia, one of the most difficult areas we relate to, and work with our IMB missionaries and strategic partners.

Every church, every class, every small group should view itself as a sending post. Whether you have 30 people or 1,000, they are potential missionaries to serve the nations. So issue the call to them! Use the

> Every church, every class, every small group should view itself as a sending post. Whether you have 30 people or 1,000, they are potential missionaries to serve the nations.

number of people God has entrusted to you and make the most of them for His kingdom. Don't use church size as an excuse for disobedience. It's not our size; it's the Lord we serve. He gives us the provision to do what He calls us to do.

If you've got a chance to go to an unreached people and it feels like you're in way over your head, find a few other churches to join you in taking a piece of the ministry. The more the better. You *want* others to be involved; it's a good thing. You're multiplying your influence rather than playing the Lone Ranger. Even the Lone Ranger needed Tonto. The go-it-alone mentality hurts international missions just like it hurts church planting in the United States. "Well, we can't start churches like Woodstock does," someone will say. Sure you can! If you're a smaller church, partner with four or five other churches and do it. Believe in the people you are leading, be unselfish and see what happens. What have you got to lose? Your people? If you're holding them that close, you're not discipling them biblically.

Pastors often tell me, "Johnny, I'm so busy. I'm trying to make time for my family. I'm trying to get my sermons ready. I'm doing all this counseling and all this crisis response. I'm going to all these meetings. I don't have time for missions."

I try to teach young pastors to discover and develop their main gifts, their strengths, and then find lay people, or as the church grows, bring on staff who are stronger in those areas and let them exercise their gifts. There are things I'm just not good at. I let someone else do them. Find a lay person. The people in the church will let you do it all if you will, but they will help you do it if you make it a "we" rather than an "I" ministry.

One of the great church leadership statements is this: *People need to turn leadership back over to the leaders. Leaders need to turn ministry back over to the people.* We see the biblical principle in Exodus 18, where Jethro, the father-in-law of Moses, basically said to Moses, "If you continue to do ministry the way you're doing it, you will wear out, and the people with you will wear out also." He told Moses to find the best leaders among the Israelites and put 1,000 people under them. The next-best leaders got groups of 100, then 50, right on down to 10.

You can preach all you want about reaching the world for Christ, but if you don't get out there on the edge with your people, they won't go. Go with them!

If you turn the ministry over to your people, you'll be amazed at what they do.

START LOCALLY

The light that shines the farthest shines the brightest at home.

If you love your Jerusalem, you will love the ends of the earth—and vice versa. It has to start at home. We have high school students who want to go on a mission trip to the Dominican Republic, but those students must go out to the community here before they go there. It's part of their discipleship. We'll say, "You're not gonna go and share Jesus in the Dominican Republic if you're not sharing Him here, so we'll see ya at visitation this week!"

We live in the third-largest nation of lostness. As I said before, India and China are the only nations that have more lost people than the United States. Atlanta is one of the most multicultural cities in the United States. We're working in the international community on the east side of Atlanta. There are anywhere from 35 to 40 language groups in a two-square-mile area. We have unpaid staff members leading the charge there, doing Upward Basketball in a refugee community, summer camps, sports clinics, and other ministries, trying to reach that community for Christ.

A major function we do each year is an International Thanksgiving Festival. Last year we had 800 people from 31 nations on the property for Thanksgiving. We try to find out where they come from beforehand and be ready to give them *JESUS* films and copies of God's Word in their languages. About 200 of our people gave up their Thanksgiving meal to come "serve the nations"—literally—cooking and preparing meals for them.

There's a low-income area where the majority of the residents are Latino. We've been going to feed them and preach the Gospel every week for the last 10 years at least. We call it "Church on the Street." About 40 of our people go, from medical doctors to plumbers to teenagers. They go 51 weeks out of the year—rain, sleet, or snow—because the people will be on the streets.

During our "Love Loud" week of outreach this year, about 2,500 of our people gave about $1 million worth of free services to the community. Six dentists and two oral surgeons gave free dental care starting at 8 a.m. People started showing up at 4 o'clock in the morning. We had five or six medical doctors giving free physicals and prescriptions. We fed all the firefighters and police in Cherokee County. We did free car care in our parking lot for widows, single moms, and seniors. We did free home repairs. Home Depot gave us thousands and thousands of dollars worth of lumber and sheetrock when they found out what we were doing. It rained like crazy that week, but it never dampened their spirits!

We're trying to get our people to adopt or take in foster kids. Our goal in another year or so is to train enough church families to accommodate every foster child in the county. We've been working in the jails for 15 years.

This year we launched an eight-week study on Christianity and Islam. We want to educate our people about Islam and about their own Bible to equip them to engage Muslims in Atlanta, in their own neighborhoods, their workplaces, in the schools, and on the college campuses.

START!

I could go on and on, but I've gone to braggin'. It's 24/7 around Woodstock. There's something happening all the time. We try to keep it really "hot" so we're always engaging the local community, our nation, and the nations.

> Catch God's heart, and He will take you and your people to some amazing places!

You can do that, too. But you've got to start somewhere. Don't feel equipped? Do it anyway and learn as you go.

People are smarter than we give them credit for. Especially young people—they're so perceptive. They know whether or not you care, which is what really counts. Humble yourself; they know your weaknesses anyway. If you want to move your church toward missions but you're not there yourself, admit it to your people.

We try to keep it really "hot" at Woodstock so we're always engaging the local community, our nation, and the nations. You can do that, too. But you've got to start somewhere. Don't feel equipped? Do it anyway and learn as you go. You teach what you know. You reproduce who you are.

Tell them, I've been trying to teach this, but it's not who I am—yet. It's who I *want* to be. I'm asking God to change me, to change us, and I want us to do this *together*. I'm not speaking as one who knows all the answers but as a brother who is struggling with you. I want to tell you what I'm learning in my journey. People love vulnerability and they respect honesty. They will go anywhere with you if they know you are walking right beside them.

You teach what you know. You reproduce who you *are*. Catch God's heart, and He will take you and your people to some amazing places!

*John Piper, Let the Nations be Glad! The Supremacy of God in Missions, 2nd ed. (Grand Rapids, MI: Baker Academic, 2003), 1.

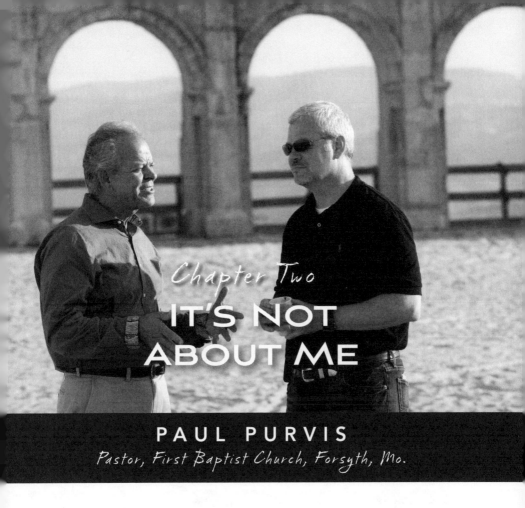

Chapter Two
IT'S NOT ABOUT ME

PAUL PURVIS
Pastor, First Baptist Church, Forsyth, Mo.

When I was a kid, I had a "drug" problem: I was drug to church Sunday morning, Sunday night, Monday night, Wednesday night—you get the picture.

You've probably heard that old preacher's joke, but it pretty accurately describes my upbringing—an upbringing I'm thankful for. I grew up in a pastor's home with parents who loved the Lord and loved me and my brother. I became a follower of Christ at the age of 7, and there's never been any doubt in my mind it was a clear moment of conversion in my heart.

I grew up learning God's Word in "Bible Drills," going to Royal Ambassador camp every summer, and later being a camp counselor in South Carolina, my home state. Family vacations? You guessed it—going to the annual Southern Baptist Convention. My dad, Don Purvis, was pastor of the same church in South Carolina for 32 years. He's a hero to me, a great and godly man.

In short, every step of my early life was about as Southern Baptist as you can get. What's more, you could not have grown up more "mission-minded" than I did.

And yet, this is what "mission-minded" meant to me: God calls some people to go to China or Africa, and I'll pray for them and give to support them during Lottie Moon Christmas Offering® and Annie Armstrong Easter Offering® time. It never really occurred to me that missionaries on the field—and the local Christians they work with—needed or wanted a partnership with churches like ours. Missionaries had come to speak at our church for as long as I could remember, but did I really have an awareness of God's wider world and my relationship to it? The answer is no.

What changed? Read on.

THROUGH THE VALLEY

I wanted to serve God with my life, but I had no clear call to vocational ministry as a young person. Dad always told me (and my brother, who also became a pastor), "If there's anything else you can do and be happy, do it!" I felt that I had gifts and abilities in other areas, so I went to Furman University in Greenville, S.C., to study political science. I had some great opportunities to serve in student government and in Washington on the late Sen. Strom Thurmond's staff. I thought I had everything mapped out—where I was going to law school, what I was going to do, how I was going to make the jump into politics.

Everything changed when I was a junior in college. One night I knelt down beside my bed and surrendered all my plans to God. I knew by then that He was calling me to serve Him vocationally. The details of my future became a lot muddier, but the peace in my heart was clearer than it had ever been. That night a journey with God began that led me to Southwestern Baptist Theological Seminary. The first day there I met the woman who would become my wife. Kimberly was beginning her seminary education, too, and together we started walking the path where God was leading us.

We had the privilege of serving some great churches in Texas, Alabama, Georgia, and Florida before coming to First Baptist Church of Forsyth, Mo., in 2006. I've seen God move in wonderful ways. I've also struggled with my own weaknesses.

The challenges of being a pastor are manifold. The overarching one, for a God-called man, is the conviction that this is a call I want to fulfill faithfully. Put that together with a "Type A" personality like mine, and you've got a strong drive to do your best. But that drive can get you into trouble when you lose God's perspective.

It's exciting to think, I can go out there and be used of God to grow a church. The pressure comes when you start thinking, wow, *I've* got to grow a church. If you're not careful, you can forget that it is God who grows His church—not you. We're to be available, we're to give it our all, but we have to depend on Him for the results.

I don't know if I've learned that lesson entirely, but I learned part of it by walking through the valley. For a time, I did not handle the stress and challenge of ministry well.

Through that process, I learned an important life principle: God is my sustenance. That helps you not only in ministry but in marriage, in family life, in relationships, in every aspect of your life. We're in it for Him, and it's all for His glory. Seek His Kingdom and His righteousness, as Jesus says in Matthew 6, and don't worry about anything else. That's the real challenge we wake up to every day.

During those years of struggle, I was especially grateful that I had built a relationship with Johnny Hunt and began to be mentored by his leadership. He played an integral role in helping me walk through this valley in ministry.

I remember reading an article about what God was doing in his ministry at First Baptist Woodstock and the revolutionary change in the church there. I thought, OK, I've got to make an effort to connect there.

My brother and I were in Atlanta years ago, and I said, "Let's ride out and see this Woodstock church." We drove out to Woodstock with no appointment, went by the office, and asked if someone could show us around. Dan Dorner, the pastor of administration, spent several hours with us talking about the church, sharing what God was doing there, and answering every question we had. We walked away saying to ourselves, "Man, if a leader has surrounded himself with this kind of staff member, that's the kind of leader we want to get to know."

The following year I attended my first Timothy+Barnabas conference at Woodstock—the first of many. Timothy+Barnabas serves two functions: to equip pastors and to encourage pastors. You sit under Johnny Hunt's teaching and you realize he has so much wisdom to offer. But he also makes you feel uplifted and encouraged in ministry, because ministry can be very discouraging. The first year I went by myself—didn't know any better. I wasn't there very long before I realized this is a conference for pastors and their wives. "Miss Janet" Hunt comes

What kind of legacy do I want to leave? Is it just what I can accomplish in one community or several communities in a local church setting? The day is going to come when nobody in those communities will even remember my name.

alongside Johnny to encourage wives and equip them to deal with what it means to be a pastor's wife and the struggles they face. It has helped Kimberly and me tremendously.

That's the kind of pastor Johnny Hunt is. He cares about people. As a young pastor at that first conference, I realized he wouldn't just give me a glance and walk off. He was willing to sit and talk. Over time, he was willing to invest deeply in my life. You want to learn from somebody like that. You want to grow from that kind of discipling process.

Relationships of any kind are hard work. Ultimately, though, I've got to ask myself: What kind of legacy do I want to leave? Is it just what I can accomplish in one community or several communities in a local church setting? The day is going to come when nobody in those communities will even remember my name. But if I can invest in the lives of other people, who invest in the lives of others, who invest in the lives of others—and if that investment involves communicating the Gospel around God's world—*that* is a legacy that will continue for eternity.

That's the kind of legacy building Johnny Hunt taught me. And that's how I became more personally involved in missions.

TRANSFORMATIONAL MOMENT

I had been on international mission trips. But when Johnny invited me to go with him to Argentina, the experience exposed me to missions in a different way than I had ever seen. For the first time, I had an opportunity to walk hand in hand with local believers whose lives had been transformed—and who had their own passion to see God's Good News spread around the world. I began to realize not only that these people desired a connection with us, but what they were already doing was awesome. I wanted our people back home to be connected with them. I thought, we can do this as a church.

That trip became a transformational moment in my ministry. As a pastor, I also began to understand I had to help our people personalize missions. I began to use the Global Impact Celebration model, where we bring missionaries to our church to help personalize their work, then take our people to international settings to get them involved in missions.

Our church, First Baptist of Forsyth, is located just outside of Branson, Mo., a tourist city that has 8 million visitors a year. Forsyth is a small town of 1,600 people. The church sits between the two on a two-lane country road. When God called us here, First Baptist had already developed into a good-sized church for a rural area. On a typical Sunday we may have 700 people in worship, so we're not a mega-church, but we're growing.

More importantly, we're focused on seeing those who don't know Christ come to Him. In that sense I serve one of the best churches in the world, because we really don't play "church games." We saw 128 baptisms last year because we try to do whatever it takes to reach those who aren't being reached. That's why I'm there.

> We've continued to see the excitement grow.
> We've continued to see our people give.
> But now we are also *going*.

My first year at First Baptist, I introduced the Global Impact Celebration. We brought in 15 missionary families from our area and around the world, including several IMB families. That first year, we saw our total missions giving quadruple. We have a long way to go, but it's changed the way the church sees the world. We've continued to see the excitement grow. We've continued to see our people give. But now we're also *going*.

We now have at least one consistent, ongoing mission partnership project internationally. We're working in France to reach students for Christ. We're talking with our IMB workers about how to connect with them to reach the large Muslim population there. We're sending

Believers in other lands are hungry for us to come alongside them and help them learn from our experiences. If you broaden your horizons beyond your local setting, you will realize that as your people go to the nations and share, they will come back energized to accomplish the task at home.

mission teams to other places, too. It's refreshing to be able to challenge our people to have a Great Commission mindset.

I pastor a Southern Baptist church, but most of our newer people don't really know what that means from a historical or denominational viewpoint. They just know they want to be Great Commission followers of Jesus Christ. But when I go to a place like the Middle East, see the work missionaries are doing, and talk about ways we can partner, I get excited about saying to our folks, "Look at the way your denomination is helping reach those who don't know Christ"—even if we aren't limited by denomination in our overall ministry.

I visited several Middle Eastern countries with Johnny Hunt in 2009. We taught and prayed with pastors from six nations in the region, visited our IMB missionaries there—and experienced the sheer spiritual darkness of the region.

One morning we stood on a rooftop in a largely Muslim city and listened to the Islamic call to Friday prayers. The preaching in the mosques all over the city was broadcast into the streets. It was an overwhelming experience to realize that the Muslim preachers were unashamedly—in fact, extremely boldly—communicating what they view as truth and what we know is a lie. The competing voices filled the valley where the city is located. It was a sound of confusion, but our God is not a God of confusion. The Bible says Jesus came that we might have peace, a peace that surpasses all human understanding.

It was disheartening to realize that while falsehood is being spread, the Light is not shining in this darkness. It was like walking into pitch-black night and meeting so many who can't see. I, too, once was blind, but now I see. I've experienced the Light in my life, so my burden is to help those around me who are searching. I know they were created with the very same God-shaped void in their hearts.

The Northern African and Middle Eastern peoples need to understand the *truth*, and they can only do that if they hear the truth. According to God's Word, we are the ones to help take the truth to them. We need to do whatever it takes to communicate the Good News of Jesus Christ in that part of the world, so the truth that changes lives will overwhelm the confusion we heard that morning.

'SHEEP LOOK LIKE THE SHEPHERD'

We have many reasons to be proud as a denomination. Sometimes I wonder if we are not too prideful. On that rooftop in the Middle East, we seemed very small. There is much to be done. We can't do it alone. We can't do it the way we have been doing it, and we can't do it with the resources that we've been sending. We all have to do more, give more, go more, and pray more. We have to be sensitive to what God is calling us to do. God is calling many of us sitting at home to go.

The pastor sets the tone. As Johnny says, "Eventually the sheep begin to look like the shepherd." If I have a heart for missions, our people are going to get a heart for missions. It may not happen overnight, but eventually it begins to breed within them.

I've also seen that believers in other lands are hungry for folks to come alongside them and help them learn from our experiences, our successes, and our failures. They have the same struggles, and though there may be cultural barriers, we can break down those walls and relate to each other. If you, as a pastor in the United States, will broaden your horizon and step away from that local ministry setting for a moment, you will realize that as your people go to the nations and share, they will come back more equipped, more excited, and more energized to accomplish the task at home.

A truth I've heard for many years (it's one of Johnny's favorites) is this: The light that shines the farthest shines the brightest at home. Often we get so consumed with our little part of the world that we don't branch out. Yet if a pastor will take the time to reach beyond his church walls, not only in the community but in the world, it will change his whole view of ministry. It refreshes you and recharges you in the area of local ministry. I've been in the metropolitan church setting and in the smaller setting, and it's easy to be overwhelmed no matter where you serve. But when you walk the streets of the Middle East or Paris and realize the vast lostness of the world, it puts your individual task into better perspective.

Several things take place. First, you realize you don't have a choice but to help reach the lost of the world. This really is a heaven-and-hell issue. If we don't come together and attempt to make a difference, millions of people are heading to hell without hope of eternal life. The local church's role in missions is not only commissioned in Acts 1:8, it's modeled throughout the book of Acts. Paul challenged individual churches at every turn to get involved.

Secondly, you realize, wow, nothing excites my people like hands-on missions. When they get excited about that, they not only do the things they should be doing in the life of the body, they stop doing the things they *shouldn't* be doing, whether that's grumbling or gossiping or getting sidetracked into trivial issues.

When your eyes are opened to the vastness and the lostness of the world, you're faced with the reality that you can't afford to keep

I don't think we need more education in the church. We need more obedience.

playing "church games." We don't have time for that. We've got to do everything we can to make a difference. When you truly become broken and realize it isn't about you, it's easier to have a missions mindset. If my focus is being the next big church or the next guy on a speaking circuit or moving up a ladder, if I'm driven by that kind of Western "success" mindset in ministry, then there's no way I'll take time to go to the darkest areas, where they don't care who I am.

Sometimes our eyes are opened internationally, sometimes locally. I've noticed the greatest change in people at First Baptist through a local project we're doing. Hundreds of our people are involved, and in a lifetime of church activity, I've never seen lay people so excited about ministering and serving. So whether folks catch a heart for missions "over here" or "over there," once they catch it, it's going to spread out both ways. It's an opportunity for them to do what we've been telling them to do, however long they've been coming to church.

You see, I don't think we need more education in the church. We need more obedience. But we can't expect our people to be obedient if we pastors aren't obedient. We can't expect our people to be faithful to do their part in the Great Commission if our vision is limited to our Jerusalem. In most cases, we don't even go to our Jerusalem; we limit ourselves to the walls that contain the church facilities in our Jerusalem.

I don't think I'd have the heart to reach my community if I didn't have a heart for God's world. I don't think I would be so passionate, not about growing a church or "swapping sheep," but about reaching lost people. That's an outflow of a missions heart. *It's not about me.* It's about God and bringing Him more worshippers. It's about the ones who need Him, whether they're Muslim or Hindu or Buddhist. They have the same God-shaped void as that person in the Ozarks or in Georgia or in South Carolina. And they can't know about Him unless somebody is bold enough to talk to them. And we can't talk to them if we're not there.

I want to be there, and I want my church to be there. What about you?

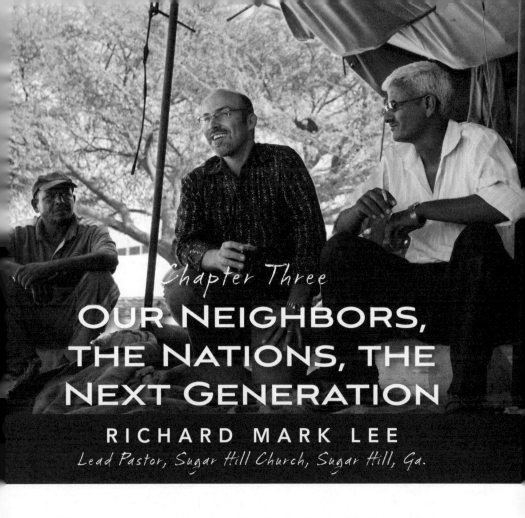

Chapter Three
OUR NEIGHBORS, THE NATIONS, THE NEXT GENERATION
RICHARD MARK LEE
Lead Pastor, Sugar Hill Church, Sugar Hill, Ga.

Times have changed for churches. Radically. And it didn't take long.

I'm 39, and I've always been part of the church scene. My dad was a Southern Baptist music minister, so I was born one Sunday and in church the next. A lot of the kids I grew up with were the same way, whether their parents were in ministry or not. We're in the heart of the Bible Belt in Georgia, after all. Most everybody used to go to church around here.

That was then. This is now: A 50-year-old man in our town recently asked, "Do you have to close your eyes and fold your hands to pray?" He wasn't challenging me or being sarcastic; he honestly didn't know.

I'm pastor of Sugar Hill Church in Sugar Hill, Ga., northeast of Atlanta. About 15,500 people live here. If you add Buford and Suwanee, our neighboring towns, nearly 50,000 folks live in the area. Suwanee gets the name recognition, and Buford is more well-established; Sugar Hill is more of a bedroom community to metro Atlanta.

Twenty years ago this was a country town. One lady in our church told me, "Before all you 'foreigners' moved here, our phone numbers were only four digits!" People have moved here from all over the world. Fourteen different nations are represented in our church. I wish that meant we were truly multicultural in our ministry. We're not there yet, but we're working on it.

> ## We're still in the Bible Belt by perception, but we live in a spiritually lost area.

Our demographics have drastically changed—economically, ethnically, and spiritually. According to statistics, 88 percent of the people in our community do not attend church even once a month. We're still in the Bible Belt by perception, but we live in a spiritually lost area. I served on jury duty last year, and one of the questions they asked us was, "Do you attend religious services at least once a month?" Only about 15 percent of us said yes, which confirmed the statistics for me.

We run into a lot of indifference—and even some hostility—in the community. That's why we have made an intentional effort to get away from the "Baptist" label. We're not ashamed of our doctrine or who we are, but we're trying to break down some of the animosity that is not necessarily directed toward Jesus and the Gospel. Maybe someone has been hurt by church people in the past or has negative perceptions of Baptists. We began as First Baptist Church of Sugar Hill, yet I sat in a living room with someone who said, "I will *never* go back to a First Baptist Church"—any First Baptist, anywhere. I said, "Well, let's have a conversation about Jesus, not Baptists."

DOERS NOT SPECTATORS

I share all this because it affects what we do in ministry and missions at home and around the world. If you're a pastor, I'm guessing you deal with some of the same dynamics—regardless of how deep in the old Bible Belt you might be.

God called me to Sugar Hill in 2001, and if the Lord allows me to stay, I don't have aspirations to go anywhere else. I'm not shifting into neutral by any stretch; I just see all the dreams the Lord has given me coming to fruition here, even if they're coming in little baby steps.

I want to reach our culture and reach our generation. I want to see us reach northeast Georgia for the glory of God and, eventually, to have a missions partnership in every time zone and every continent on earth. Our slogan is "Our neighbors, the nations, and the next generation." We want to love our neighbors, reach the nations, and do things that outlive ourselves.

We are a church in transition. It's been a long journey and not one without some wounds. We were a very traditional First Baptist Church of about 250 to 300 members when I came nine years ago. Today we're known as Sugar Hill Church from a "branding" standpoint, and about 1,600 people attend on a good Sunday. We're growing about 10 percent

> I want to reach our culture and reach our generation. I want to see us reach northeast Georgia for the glory of God and, eventually, to have a missions partnership in every time zone and every continent on earth.

per year. We do two distinct styles of services. Our modern service is worship, celebration, smoke and lights, loud music, blue jeans, and untucked shirts. It doesn't feel much like your mama's church!

But the same missiology that says we're going to reach a new generation with that style also causes us to keep doing a service that has a more familiar feel. You can't tell people "that was yesterday and this is today" and leave all tradition behind. I can't make that fit my Bible. We're not just trying to pacify older church members but to reach new folks who need more of a traditional church setting for worship.

We preach the Bible in both services. I tell people to measure what I say against the Word of God. We give an invitation to respond to the Gospel. It may not be a "come forward" invitation, but we'll give you an opportunity every Sunday to respond to the Gospel. We haven't let go of who we are as Baptists. We are proud to be Southern Baptist in our heritage, our doctrine, and our mission.

To be frank, though, we are not loyal to an *institution*. We are passionate about the *mission* being accomplished. That goes for our church and many other churches led by pastors of my generation. The guys I know who are passionate about missions and reaching lost people are actually involved in it. The key is *personalization*.

To engage our neighbors and the nations in the next generation, we've got to get personally involved in each of those areas, not just write a check and consider it done. We're not looking to throw away anything. Let's learn from our past, but let's not keep repeating the same thing and getting the same results.

Give us an opportunity to be involved. We don't even need to lead. We just need to be involved. We're doers, not spectators sitting back and watching.

Locally, servant evangelism is Sugar Hill's priority. We say to our folks, "Invest in relationships with lost people. Don't hang out with church people all the time." We are involved with our city government and our schools; those are our local mission fields. We love the people in our community. Instead of doing a fall festival on our church campus, for example, we helped sponsor the city's festival and supplied

125 volunteers to help make it happen. So instead of having maybe 1,000 people on our campus, we were able to serve 9,000 people from all over the area.

We have a presence on seven high school campuses, including a ministry to pregnant teenage girls. School counselors are calling and

> We say to our folks, "Invest in relationships with lost people. Don't hang out with church people all the time."

saying, "These students have gotten pregnant. Can you help them?" We know of one young girl who was going to have an abortion, but because some of our adults cared about her and helped her, she decided to keep the baby.

During the weeks leading up to Christmas, we delivered a bag of coffee to every school employee in our district—6,000 bags in all. We didn't force Jesus on anyone; we just gave them a gift. Later, someone may call and say, "I have a problem in my marriage, and your church gave me a gift one time. Can you help me?" When they have crises, I become the pastor to people who have no church. We're breaking down barriers.

PERSONALIZING THE BIG PICTURE

When it comes to our involvement in world missions, personalization is just as important—maybe even more so.

The folks God is bringing in our doors couldn't care less about a denominational label. They couldn't care less about an institution. They just want to grow, to find out who Jesus is, what He's like, and how we can serve Him together. *Then* they'll do missions, but they want to do it personally. Every year when we talk about Lottie Moon,

I am asked, "Haven't we paid her off yet?" They'll give to a specific cause or to a person, but they have a hard time understanding the big picture of missions.

We need to put a name and a face on it. To say we have 5,000 missionaries around the world means nothing to our people. But to say here's John and Jane Smith, who live in this specific city, which is the gateway to this unreached people group, and have our people visit them and maybe have them visit us, gives us a personal connection. We also see that we can not only support John and Jane and their team, but now we understand a little more about the hundreds of other missionaries in their region. Now it's become personalized, because we have connected the dots.

We took 50 people to the Middle East several years ago, and that really got us going. We worked alongside one of our IMB missionaries I knew from college, so there was a relational connection. I took my family to a major city there and watched my two school-age daughters hand out Bibles door to door. That was awesome!

Then we shifted our focus to Kenya, where we were able to plant two churches. We trained pastors in partnership with the mother church there, and those two churches have multiplied to 19 churches as they have taken the Gospel to neighboring villages. We poured ourselves into that work for about three years, and we've still got a few folks

> We've had some starts and stops in missions. We've had some failures. I've been discouraged and ready to give up at times.

keeping it going. A layman in our church literally has quit his job and raised his own support to be a "connector" for that ministry. He's in Kenya six or eight times a year developing relationships.

We need to put a name and a face on missions. To say we have 5,000 missionaries around the world means nothing to our people. But now that we've been there, it's become personalized. We know them. We know the people we are trying to reach. We have connected the dots.

I'll be real honest, though: We've had some starts and stops in missions. We've had some failures. I've been discouraged and ready to give up at times. Beyond that, the national economic crisis hit our community hard. A lot of our folks are in the construction industry, so when that bubble burst, it certainly affected us. About 18 percent of our church members are either unemployed or significantly under-employed.

But Johnny Hunt's leadership has reengaged me to be more passionate about where we are headed as a denomination. From a missions standpoint, he has probably made the single greatest impact on my life as a pastor.

When I came to Sugar Hill as pastor, I sent letters to 11 key Southern Baptist pastors in the greater Atlanta area, basically saying, "I'm a 30-year-old kid. I'd be honored if you'd give me an hour." Johnny Hunt responded. A couple of others did, too, but from that moment, Johnny kind of took me under his wing. He has sought me out, probably twice a year, to come do something with him. He has taken a personal interest in me as a pastor. Because of that, I follow his leadership.

Johnny's nothing like me. We're a generation apart in style, in the structure of our churches, and so forth. But I have the greatest respect and admiration for him, and I want to be found faithful in following the path he has paved for people like me to carry the banner of missions. If I can be to others what Johnny is in his circle of influence, I'd be

> When our church goes back to that country
> on a vision trip, we will sit down with our
> missionaries and ask, "How can we come alongside
> you? How can we help you fulfill your vision?"

well-pleased. I'm 39, and I surely don't have it all figured out, but now I've got half a dozen pastors who are calling me, wanting to know how we've grown and what's happening with us. So instead of being so self-consumed, I pause and give them all the time they ask for, because Johnny certainly has done that for me.

He invited me to go with him to several countries in the Middle East in 2009. We taught at a conference with Baptist pastors from six countries in the region. Politically, their nations are fighting with each other, so to watch these guys pray together and see that God is bigger than war and conflict was very moving. I've been in contact via e-mail with two or three of them since the trip, and we've developed a friendship and prayer network.

The highlight of the trip for me was a one-day seminar for all the Southern Baptist workers in one of the countries in the Middle East. To meet with them, to see them, and then to visit some of their ministries made me more passionate about their task. Frankly, I've promoted the Lottie Moon Christmas Offering® more because of it. When our church goes back to that country on a vision trip, we will sit down with our missionaries and ask, "How can we come alongside you? How can we help you fulfill your vision?" We'll also support and pray for them like never before.

Now I've got a vision that's easy to communicate to our church. Maybe we can help lead some other churches to partner overseas, too, and make missions more personal for them. I am prouder to be Southern Baptist than I ever have been. I am very proud of our missionaries and what they are doing on the field. Frankly, my eyes have been opened, because I was probably on the fence for a while about Southern Baptist missions. But now I know them. I can name them. I've met with them. I've seen them in action.

If we cut off the lost of the world because of economics, woe to us for being disobedient to Christ's command. I can't stand before God or my people with integrity and say, "We need to ignore these and take care of our own."

Through Johnny Hunt, we've also developed a relationship with southern Brazil. We've sent maybe two dozen folks there over the last couple of years, and I've participated in a couple of "Timothy+Barnabas" conferences at Johnny's invitation to train Latin American pastors for international missions. We work in a community in Porto Alegre, Brazil, where less than 1 percent of the people claim to be Christian. It's very rough, very poor, very hardened. There's a witchcraft mentality mixed with cultural Catholicism. Teenagers are into drugs and sex because they have nothing else to do. We work in a couple of "cardboard cities" that will break your heart. We go into government-run schools that allow our youth to come in and tell their story about life in America— and about their personal faith.

MISSIONS: NOT AN OPTION

A lot of supposedly evangelistic churches don't venture very far from home. But when someone tells me we shouldn't be running around the world when 88 percent of the people right around Sugar Hill are lost, my answer is that Jesus didn't give us an option.

Yes, in a tough economy we have to make some hard decisions, and it's easier to cut the ministries and people we're not looking at eyeball to eyeball every day. But we have to answer this question: Are we being obedient to the stewardship of the Gospel? If we cut off the lost of the world because of economics, woe to us for being disobedient to Christ's command. I can't stand before God or my people with integrity and say, "We need to ignore these and take care of our own."

Some older folks still ask, "Why spend the money to go overseas yourself when you ought to just put that money in the offering plate for missions?" My response is, "Your generation did that. But my generation is going in person, and they are going to give *more* because they went."

I'm not a big theologian, but I do believe we're in the last days. I want to make the biggest difference I can for the kingdom of God. Instead of coasting, let's give our all while we can, because one day He's going to call us home. I want to take as many people with us as we can. Heaven's gonna be a party, but we have only a short time to invite people, so let's spend all of our time reaching out.

We'll work on the other stuff when we get there!

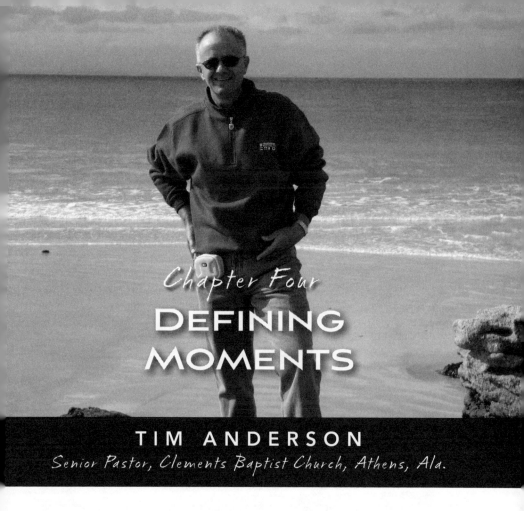

Chapter Four
DEFINING MOMENTS

TIM ANDERSON
Senior Pastor, Clements Baptist Church, Athens, Ala.

Have you heard the song "Defining Moment" by NewSong, my favorite Christian group? The lyrics tell about those moments that come in the life of every believer—and every church.

> *"There comes a time, in every heart*
> *a time of real decision*
> *when we reach the point of choosin'*
> *how we would live our lives.*
> *All our hopes, all our dreams*
> *will rise up from that moment,*
> *the moment we surrender,*
> *and choose to follow Christ. ...*

When you believe He's all you need
that will be your defining moment.
As you live your life walking in His light,
trusting Him completely,
that will be,
that will be,
your defining moment. ... "

What a message! NewSong gave us permission several years ago to use "Defining Moment" as the theme song for our radio and television ministry at Clements Baptist Church in Athens, Ala., where I've been pastor since 1994. When I heard that song for the first time, I had just returned from a retreat in the mountains, and I'd been thinking about that very phrase—defining moment. God was speaking to me out of 2 Corinthians 5:17: "Therefore if anyone is in Christ, there is a new creation; old things have passed away, and look, new things have come." I thought, when a man meets Christ, that is his defining moment.

I've experienced a number of defining moments in my life. Let me tell you about a few of them, because they explain why our church has a passion for reaching the world with the Gospel today.

The first and most important occurred when I was 10 years old. I came to know Christ on a Friday morning in Vacation Bible School in Athens, where I grew up. I really believed the preacher was talking to me when he said that Jesus wanted to save me. I didn't go forward because my friends did. I went forward because I felt a tug in my heart. He called; I answered.

The second-best decision I ever made was to marry my high school sweetheart, Sherry, when we were both 19. We celebrated 30 years of marriage in 2009. We have three great children, a wonderful son-in-law and daughter-in-law—and the best granddaughter in the world!

I didn't go into full-time church ministry in the early years of our life together. In fact, I worked for General Motors for more than 18 years. During the last five, I was a bi-vocational pastor, but that's getting ahead of the story. At the GM plant, I worked in what we called the heat-and-treat area where steel was prepared for the manufacturing process.

Sherry and I served our church family at First Baptist Church in Athens, where I was a Sunday School teacher and deacon.

How did I know God was calling me to preach? That's a question every pastor asks, and it was another defining moment for me. First of all, I knew I couldn't be happy doing anything else. First Timothy 3:1 says, "... If anyone aspires to be an overseer, he desires a noble work." I believe God gives you that desire, but at the same time, I knew I had the human desire to serve Him as a preacher. Ten years earlier, I wouldn't even lead a public prayer in church. I was intimidated. Even when I started teaching a college and career class, I would be intimidated when they talked about things like Saul's conversion in Acts 9. I didn't even know who Saul was. I was biblically challenged.

Even though I knew I was born again, I was *not* an obvious candidate to be a preacher. I thought, only God can do this! But I knew the Lord was reconstructing my whole life. I started going to extension classes through Samford University and later New Orleans Baptist Theological Seminary. I'm still working on some of my academic goals and putting things together as best I can. I left First Baptist in 1990 and went to my first church as a bi-vocational pastor, Concord Baptist Church on the eastern side of Limestone County. I stayed there for three and a half years before coming to Clements in 1994.

'YOU'LL NEVER GO BACK'

Clements Baptist Church is a church plant. Our associational director of missions at that time believed there was a need for a church on the west side of the county. With the help of the association and a mother church, a core of people put together a plan and obtained the land. I was still with GM when I came to Clements as pastor. The church was starting to grow, and they called me as full-time pastor after the first year and a half. Another defining moment had come for me, and it involved a huge step of faith.

General Motors might not be doing so well today, but back in those days a GM job was *the* job to have in our corner of Alabama. I made good money. I had incredible benefits. But it was not what I was supposed to do anymore—and I knew it. Sherry and I prayed through it, but we didn't have to pray long.

I'll never forget my last day on the job. I had a good relationship with plant management, so I was granted a 90-day leave of absence to decide if being a pastor was what I really wanted to do. As I was leaving the house around 6 that morning, Sherry looked at me and said, "You'll never go back."

"Beg your pardon?" I replied.

"You'll never go back," she repeated.

"Well, not for a while," I agreed. "I've got a 90-day leave, and I'm gonna use it."

"I understand that," she answered patiently. "But you are leaving our home today to go back to that plant for the last time."

Sherry was a prophet. I never went back. She knew God's call on my life and has been part of it from the beginning.

God started our church with 45 people. Now we average 700 in attendance. We celebrated 15 years at Clements in October 2009, and God has done more than I could ever imagine or dream. Our church family is unparalleled. They are incredible people. We're in a rural area that will grow a lot over the next 10 years, but it's still a farming area now.

'JERUSALEM'

My main gifts are encouragement, exhortation, and just loving people. I'm committed to expository preaching of the Word and teaching our folks the importance of the Great Commission.

Our church is built upon the foundation of Psalm 126:6: "Though one goes along weeping, carrying the bag of seed, he will surely come back with shouts of joy, carrying his sheaves." We believe that—and we practice it. Outreach is a challenge for many churches these days. Not

> Not a month goes by that I don't talk with some pastor who says, "We just can't get our folks engaged in evangelism."

a month goes by that I don't talk with some pastor who says, "We just can't get our folks engaged in evangelism," or "I'm afraid to ask my people to give over a night to organized evangelism."

But it's been in our DNA at Clements from the first day. We are an outreach church. Monday night outreach is how our church began. I would go visiting with two of our key deacons, Tim Page and Jimmy Downs. Actually, they were the only deacons we had at the time. We were committed that every Monday night—no matter what—we were going out. We've gone more to a Sunday School team approach in recent years, but it's not uncommon even now to have 75 or 100 people show up on a Monday night for outreach.

We also do a "community blitz" about three times a year. We'll pick a Saturday, pray for pretty weather, target certain subdivisions, and blanket the community. I'll knock on a door and say, "Hey, I'm Tim. I'm from Clements Baptist Church, and I want to know if you have a church home." If the opportunity to share Christ arises, we do it. If not, we invite 'em to church, leave 'em a bag of goodies, and go to the next house. That might sound old school, but it still works in our area.

In Acts 1:8, Jesus says: "... you will be My witnesses in Jerusalem, in all Judea and Samaria, and to the ends of the earth." Our Acts 1:8 strategy is pretty simple. For us, "Jerusalem" is about a 10-mile radius from the church. Our "Judea and Samaria" stretches to the end of the county on both sides. Our "ends of the earth" is just that—but I'm jumping ahead again.

Our folks love outreach. We celebrate it. I recently told our church we'll succeed in the Great Commission or fail in everything else. We're not going to be an event-run church. We exist for others. We exist to share the love of Christ. When it comes to mission trips, one of my statements is, "If you're not going across the street to share the Gospel, then you're not prepared to go across the water to share the Gospel." You do it at home before you do it anywhere else. So "Jerusalem" is very important.

But we had a shortcoming as a church in earlier days. It's the same problem facing many churches: We weren't going "to the ends of the earth." We were a strong "Jerusalem" church, but we weren't doing anything internationally.

That changed when I got to know Johnny Hunt. Talk about a defining moment!

'TO THE ENDS OF THE EARTH'

For years I took our church folks to "Real Evangelism" conferences at First Baptist Woodstock in Georgia. We would have a great time and hear all the guest preachers and singers. It was one of the highlights of our year, and we fell in love with Pastor Johnny's preaching. One of the years we were there, I wandered into the administrative area. I saw Ruth Blakney, Pastor Johnny's secretary, standing at his office door. I could tell she was engaged in conversation with him, so I asked her if I could speak to him. She ushered me right in.

Pastor Johnny may not even remember that day, but he was so gracious and kind to me. He treated me like his best friend though he had known me for only 30 seconds. A year or two later, I got bold enough to ask him to preach at my church. He couldn't come on that particular Sunday, but he never made me feel like he was too busy. We found another date that worked, he came and has been a kindred spirit ever since. He preaches at Clements every year.

Nobody in the world has made a bigger impact and investment in my life than Pastor Johnny Hunt. Nobody! I've been around big-name guys in Southern Baptist circles who don't have time for you. Pastor Johnny is a different breed. He believes the calling on his life is to encourage pastors—and people in general, but especially pastors. He's one of the most giving men I've ever known—not just of his time but of his resources. Here's a man saved from the pool hall, a hellion. God saved him, arrested him, accosted him with His grace. He has never forgotten it. He loves people. He has shown me and my family nothing but the love of God. I'm a better man today as a result of knowing Johnny Hunt.

In Philippians 2:19-22, Paul wrote about sending Timothy to the Philippian church, since he had no one else of kindred spirit. Timothy, he said, "… he has served with me in the gospel ministry like a son with a father." Pastor Johnny has given me the privilege to preach for him in so many places. I used to think, well, it's not healthy to have a hero like this. Then I realized Timothy felt that way about Paul and vice versa. Paul basically said, "If I can't come, I'll send Timothy." I realized it's a biblical principle. Pastor Johnny believes if he pours his heart into pastors and mentors us, if he can't go somewhere he can send us, and it's like going himself. He can't go everywhere, but he can equip people to go in his place.

Here's how we got started in international missions. After Johnny had been coming to our church for a couple of years, I told him, "Pastor, I want to do something internationally." So he invited me to go with him to Ukraine in the former Soviet Union. I went to preach at a conference where Pastor Johnny was the keynote speaker.

I fell in love with Ukraine. The next year I took a group of our people back with me. While we were there I took a visionary look into a certain area of the country. Pastor Johnny asked, "Would you be willing to pray about partnering with missionaries to reach this area of Ukraine?" I came back and talked to my key people, and they were more than willing.

That was 2003, and we are still in partnership there. We signed a covenant with IMB missionaries at a Global Impact Celebration at our church several years ago and renewed our commitment. They've given

"Would you be willing to pray about partnering with missionaries to reach this area of Ukraine?"

us total partnership in helping us get the evangelistic task done. By the way, we've got to send more missionaries—not only because of the great ministries they have every day, but because if churches like ours don't have a missionary on the field to partner with, mission projects become very difficult. Everywhere I go, I try to find out who the closest missionaries are. We are a Southern Baptist church; I want to partner with our folks.

Pastor Johnny also introduced us to Global Focus, a mission partnership organization that connects local churches to strategic mission ministries overseas. Global Focus has helped us tremendously with our Acts 1:8 strategy. We're also involved in South Africa and Hungary through my current role as president of the International

Congress on Revival, a ministry begun by the late, great Southern Baptist evangelist Manley Beasley.

We're taking our first mission trips to Bolivia and Zimbabwe in 2010. Each year through our Global Impact Celebrations, we invite

Each time, God has opened the door through
an invitation from IMB,
Pastor Johnny, or someone else.

IMB missionaries and missionaries from other organizations to share with us. How do we determine the mission fields that are strategic for Clements? We got involved in Ukraine because we were invited. We got involved in Argentina because of an invitation. Each time, God has opened the door through an invitation from IMB, Pastor Johnny, or someone else. I didn't go out seeking it. I really believe the leadership of the Lord is more important than saying, "Lord, I'd like to go to Honduras" or wherever.

The types of mission ministry we do as a church depend on where we go. In Zimbabwe, we'll be working with schools and helping children learn the basics of English. We'll do some painting, hands-on work, reconstruction projects, and a lot of door-to-door visitation to get ready for big evangelistic meetings at night.

We believe that when the Lord leads a person in our church to go as a short-term mission volunteer, He provides the resources. It costs about $3,000 to go to Zimbabwe, for example, so we help volunteers write letters asking for faith support. First, we ask that person to put at least 10 percent of ownership into it. If it's going to cost $3,000, that is a $300 commitment. Many volunteers commit to more. Some of our teenagers may not be able to raise quite that much, but we ask them to try. We believe that gives them ownership. They're passionate about it.

But here's something God has taught me in the last few years about missions: If God wills it, God pays for it. Money will never be the reason a person cannot go. If I know somebody in particular needs some help, I get involved and go to others and say, "Hey, this guy needs another $200." God provides the support every time.

GO WITH YOUR HEART

Tough economic times have made our mission budget more of a challenge. But our folks commit to a faith promise offering, and we develop our Acts 1:8 strategy from that. It is given strictly over and above our regular tithes and mission offerings. Of course, in today's world, pastors struggle with building programs and all the other things that drive churches and church budgets. How do you build a mission-oriented church when you need to pay for all the programs and facilities at home?

> How do you build a mission-oriented church when you need to pay for all the programs and facilities at home? My response: I didn't know we had a choice. We *have* to go.

My response: I didn't know we had a choice. We *have* to go. "Jerusalem" is where we should be, but then again so is South Africa. So is Ukraine. So is Argentina.

One of the Lord's success stories in our church is Michael Browning. He was saved through our "Jerusalem" outreach ministry and became a Sunday School teacher and deacon. Through our missions conferences, God called Michael and his wife, Teresa, to be full-time IMB missionaries. They spent three years in Uruguay, South America. He's currently administrator on my staff.

But we never forget "Jerusalem." Pastor Johnny has challenged us as a convention to get involved in a "Love Loud" ministry. We believe that actions speak louder than words. James 1:22 says, "But be doers of the word and not hearers only. ..." Basically, "Love Loud" is a mission

> Every church is a direct reflection of its leadership; Pastor Johnny taught me that. I believe in people, and I believe that if you share your heart with them, if you love them, if you challenge them to love others, they'll follow you to the ends of the earth.

trip to your community. For a week, we'll ask our folks to do things like paying for lunch in the drive-through for the person behind them and sharing a Gospel tract. On another day, we're going to love and serve our city councilmen, our policemen, our nurses, our teachers. These are people who put their lives on the line for us, who teach our children, who serve our community. We'll buy them gift cards or dinner out. We'll cut grass and change the oil in vehicles for people who can't easily do it themselves.

On Saturday, we'll go to Athens and Rogersville, set up community ministry booths, and do some backyard Bible study ministry as people come through. On Sunday, we'll celebrate it all by inviting everybody to come to a Sunday night block party at one of the local ball fields. We'll cook hot dogs and hamburgers. I'll pull it all together by sharing the Gospel.

Well, that's the way we do it at Clements. God may have different ideas for you, but He wants to lead you in the same direction: His mission for His glory. If you're a pastor seeking a fresh vision from God for your people, go with what He puts in your heart.

Every church is a direct reflection of its leadership; Pastor Johnny taught me that. I believe in people, and I believe that if you share your heart with them, if you love them, if you challenge them to love others, they'll follow you to the ends of the earth.

That will be your defining moment!

Chapter Five

GOD STORY

BRAD BESSENT
Pastor, Beulah Baptist Church, Hopkins, S.C.

How does a small, rural church—one that never took a mission trip in its 200-year history—become a church that sends multiple volunteer teams to a tough part of West Africa to reach Muslims for Christ?

I don't know for sure. I still hardly believe it myself. But it happened to us, and I know it's a God thing. Some churches may be big enough to get something accomplished without God. For us, if He doesn't show up, it doesn't happen.

God has shown up at Beulah Baptist, and He has revolutionized our church. Let me tell you the story. First, though, I need to tell you some of my personal story because it illustrates how good God is.

I'm a South Carolina native. I grew up in a Presbyterian church and came to faith in Christ there. I'm sure the church influenced me, but my real salvation experience came at a church summer camp. A missionary spoke every night at camp. Toward the end of the week, he gave an altar call very much like Billy Graham. That was something that never happened at my church, and I felt God pulling on my heart. I went forward and made a decision to follow Christ. The camp turned my name into the Billy Graham Evangelistic Association, and I got follow-up Bible studies in the mail from them, filled them out, and sent them back.

I would love to say there was a real "spiritual" reason why I joined a Southern Baptist church when I was in high school. Truth is, they had a better youth ministry—and a whole lot more girls in the youth program.

I was growing in the Lord, though, and He began calling me to the ministry. There came a point when every time I prayed, God was whispering in my ear, "I want you to preach the Gospel." I fought it. I had other plans, and preaching wasn't what I wanted to do. But it got to be overwhelming. I couldn't pray; I couldn't do anything. Finally I said, "Lord, I give up. If that is what You want me to do, I'll do it."

I went off to Clemson University, still thinking deep down in my heart that I was going to get out of obeying Him. But I kept growing as a young disciple, thanks to several campus ministries and an older Baptist pastor who took me under his wing. I worked part time as a youth pastor at a church outside of Spartanburg, S.C., served for several years in another church in Spartanburg, and went to Southwestern Baptist Theological Seminary in Texas. I finished there and came back to South Carolina to pastor a new church start.

Later I went through some difficult times in my personal life. I'd tell you the whole painful story if there were space here. Suffice it to say that I lost my church, left the ministry, and spent 13 years on a spiritual roller coaster. In the midst of those dark days, Johnny Hunt invited me to come down to Woodstock and stay with him for a while. I didn't go. Looking back, I sure wish I had. Johnny has a great big heart for pastors—especially struggling pastors who need guidance and encouragement.

I had a bachelor's degree in history and a master's degree in theology. The two of those combined are worthless in the business world. The only job I could find was in sales, working on commission. I had three kids to feed, so I had no choice but to succeed in selling. After selling a little bit of everything, my wife and I bought a sign company franchise in 1998.

STARTING OVER

God didn't forget about me while I wandered in the wilderness. In fact, He stayed after me. I vividly remember the afternoon of February 5, 2004. At lunchtime, I told my wife, "I'm going home. I'm going into the study and shutting the door. God and I are going to have a long talk. If you get home and the door is still shut, just leave me alone."

For three and a half hours, God and I talked. I mostly listened. I don't even know how to describe the experience. It was an encounter with God like I'd never had before. I said, "Lord, I'll do anything You want me to do. If You want me to sell signs the rest of my life, I will. If You want me to file bankruptcy and close the doors of this business, I will. If You want me to go to Iraq, preach one message and take a bullet in the head, I'm Your guy. I'm tired of fighting You. I'm tired of running from You."

Over the next several weeks, God would wake me up about 4 a.m. I'd get up and spend two hours in prayer and Bible study. Deep down inside, the sense gradually became stronger that God was calling me back into a preaching ministry. But He just said, "For now, I want you to engage in a ministry of prayer."

I started renewing contacts with Johnny Hunt and other ministers. I had lost touch with Johnny while I was out of the ministry, but I connected with him again in 2004 just by picking up the telephone and calling him. He invited me down to spend a weekend in his home. My wife and I went and talked to him about getting back in the ministry.

On the way to church that Sunday morning, I asked him, "Johnny, do you think God can still use a hard-headed, stubborn preacher like me?" He answered, "I do!" So I said, "Where do I start?"

Johnny invited me to come back down to Woodstock for a conference, a kind of refresher course for pastors. I told him I couldn't pay for it, so he funded it—not only covering the scholarship for me to attend the conference but putting me up in a family member's home.

Other leaders helped me, too. I kept expecting people to slam the door on me, to tell me I couldn't be a pastor anymore, to forget the idea. But people kept encouraging me—especially Johnny. He still encourages me. The focus on missions and evangelism that he conveys, his continual challenge that the Great Commission stay out front, has made a strong impact on my "starting over."

God doesn't give up on His people, including prodigal sons like me. He waits for us, looks for us, and throws a big party when we come home. He restores us, renews us, and uses us for His purpose once again. And what is His purpose? That His name be glorified everywhere.

Long story short: A little church in Hopkins, S.C., named Beulah Baptist called me to be their interim pastor—twice. I accepted and served both times. In August 2005, Beulah called me as full-time pastor. We sold our business and moved to Hopkins to see what God had planned for us.

What does all this have to do with missions? Just this: God doesn't give up on His people, including prodigal sons like me. He waits for us, looks for us, and throws a big party when we come home. He restores us, renews us, and uses us for His purpose once again.

And what is His purpose? That His name be glorified everywhere.

God was gracious enough to give me a second chance, but I'm praying that I live long enough for Him to produce enough fruit through my life to make up for the years I wasted. So going to a place like West Africa was an "easy" thing for me to do because I told Him I'd go anywhere.

TURNING A BATTLESHIP

That's my personal pilgrimage back to ministry and toward missions. But the Lord worked among the people of Beulah, too. We had about 200 folks in worship when I became full-time pastor. Getting a church involved in missions is a process, and it's still playing out at Beulah. A 200-year-old church is kind of like a battleship—it doesn't turn real quick. And when it's that old, it's got a rusty rudder. If you turn it too fast, you're gonna break it.

Here's how the process unfolded for us. In 2006, I attended a session on missions partnership led by Don Brock, a pastor friend of mine, and Debbie McDowell, the missions mobilization director for the South Carolina Baptist Convention. I walked out of that meeting feeling convicted of God that I needed to be more directly involved in international missions. I called Debbie later, and she encouraged me to get Beulah involved with South Carolina's mission partnership with IMB in Southeast Asia. I looked at the distance and the cost of going that far and thought we'd never be able to do it as a small church. Little did I know at the time that it was going to cost us just as much to go to West Africa!

During the conversation, Debbie made reference to former Southern Baptist Convention President Tom Elliff, then an IMB vice president. Tom's one of my pastor heroes. I contacted him, and he put me in touch with Mike Hand and Larry Riley at IMB. We met at a coffee shop during the 2006 SBC meeting in Greensboro, N.C., and mapped out a simple mission strategy for our church on the back of an envelope.

I came back home and started preaching on missions. I also formed a "global impact team." I wrote letters to church leaders, inviting everybody to a dinner. We asked Larry Riley to come for that first meeting. More than 30 people showed up. Larry told us, "You need to

> "You need to do two things tonight. Number one, determine what 'mission' means for your church. Define it. Number two, decide how you are going to respond to Acts 1:8."

do two things tonight. Number one, determine what 'mission' means for your church. Define it. Number two, decide how you are going to respond to Acts 1:8"—where Jesus tells His followers they will be His witnesses in Jerusalem, Judea, Samaria, and to the ends of the earth.

That night, we defined mission as *engaging lostness* and *planting churches*. We defined Acts 1:8 this way: Jerusalem is our immediate community. Judea is North America. Samaria is cross-cultural outreach in America—crossing racial lines, reaching out to drug addicts or the homeless or whatever was outside our comfort zone. The ends of the earth are exactly that, no matter how far we have to go.

Then I made a recommendation: "Folks, this church is 200-plus years old, and we've been focused on Jerusalem the whole time. Why don't we start on the other end of the equation?" We agreed we would start with the ends of the earth. Larry Riley put a map up on the board and said, "Between now and the next time I come, I want you constantly looking at this map to see where God leads your eyes to fall."

That year, Southern Baptists and IMB were focusing on the hundreds of unreached people groups in West Africa that had no Gospel access, no churches, no believers. I heard descriptions of West Africa like it was the armpit of the world. Nobody wanted to go there, we were told. Missionary volunteers were decreasing, not increasing. We heard that many of the smaller unreached groups had no missionary assigned to them. IMB mission leaders were looking for local Southern Baptist churches willing to commit to reach each of these groups.

Yes, some of our folks said, "Aren't there lost people in Hopkins, S.C.? Why do we need to travel thousands of miles and spend so much money?" I have two answers to that question. One is the "nice" answer: "I agree there are a lot of lost people here. If you know a few of them, and you'll set up an appointment, I'll go with you and we'll share the Gospel with them." The "not-quite-as-nice" answer is, "Don't you think it's time other people in the world have a chance, too?"

> I heard descriptions of West Africa like it was the armpit of the world. Nobody wanted to go there, we were told.

One Sunday from the pulpit, I told the church that every year IMB has to decide, on the basis of the resources they have, which people groups are not going to get a missionary. I've listened to our missionaries say that when they make that decision, it's with a broken heart. They realize they are saying to a people group, "We're going to let you go another year without the Gospel and if you die, you're going to have to go to hell."

I wanted to illustrate that to our people, so I asked everybody in the sanctuary to stand. I asked them to imagine they were all lost without Christ. Then I said, "Only two people get to hear the Gospel out of this congregation this year. My wife and daughter are sitting out there, and obviously I love them special, so everybody else sit down except them.

Getting a church involved in missions is a process, and it's still playing out at Beulah. A 200-year-old church is kind of like a battleship—it doesn't turn real quick. Once we started turning, though, things got interesting.

I make the decision to send the Gospel to them and not to everybody else. The rest of you can just go to hell."

Two people in church that Sunday morning have never been back. When anybody asks them why, they say, "We've been going to church all our lives and never heard a preacher tell us to go to hell." That's not what I meant, of course, but that's the way they chose to hear it. I think most everybody else got the message I intended.

The night we made the commitment to go to West Africa as a church, I missed the meeting. I was recovering at home after some unexpected surgery. But our people stepped up. They were responding to God, not me. Together, we got started.

First, several of our leaders went with me to a "vision conference" on West Africa, where we met Randy Arnett, IMB mission leader for that region, and missionary Marvin Thompson. I told them we were an old, rural, blue-collar church, that we had given to the Lottie Moon Christmas Offering® and the Cooperative Program over the years, but we had never been on an international mission trip. Then I said, "We want to know where we can help you." They asked for 24 hours to think about it. The next day, they said, "We've got four people groups we want your church to pray about reaching."

Hmm. I thought. Too big a challenge for a 10,000-strong church, but he's taking *us*?

The Soninke people were their number one priority. The Bozo were number two. The third group, I don't remember. The last group was the Bambara people—who were kind of an afterthought because the IMB guys wanted to steer us toward their top recommendations. We learned that three of the groups were in the nation of Mali and that we could fly into the capital, Bamako, and visit all three—the Soninke, the Bozo, and the Bambara.

TO THE VILLAGE

In February of 2007, three laymen and I got on a plane and flew to Mali, West Africa.

Now Mali isn't exactly South Carolina, although both places have a lot of farmers and fishermen. For one thing, Mali is twice the size of Texas, with a population of more than 14 million. To the north Mali reaches deep into the Sahara Desert. The south, where most of the people live along the Niger and Senegal Rivers, has a tropical climate.

South Carolina has poverty, but not like Mali. The average Malian lives to age 50—on less than $1,000 a year. The United Nations ranks Mali's human development among the five lowest in the world. Fifty percent of Mali's infant mortality comes from malnutrition.

It's a hurting place, in other words. The people there need help, and they need the Gospel.

Without Jesus, an existence filled with hunger, suffering, illness, and hardship is the best they will ever experience. But why would they listen to what we had to say about "the white man's God?"

We had only two days scheduled for the Bambara, who were at the bottom of our "priority list." But they happened to be the first group we visited. Steve Roach, an IMB missionary assigned to the Bambara, picked us up at lunchtime our first day there.

"Bring your sleeping bag, because we're going out in the bush," Steve said. "I'm taking you to a Bambara village of 3,000. As far as I know, the Gospel has been shared only once: Two weeks ago, I went in and preached there with a group from a church that runs over 10,000 in worship."

"Aren't they going to work in the village?" I asked.

"No," Steve replied, grinning sheepishly. "They said it was too big a challenge."

Hmm, I thought. Too big a challenge for a 10,000-strong church, but he's taking *us*?

As we drove out to the village, I thought of what we'd been told about the Bambara. Four million of them live in West Africa. They claim to be 90 percent Muslim, but their Islam has been mixed with African traditional religion and superstition through the years. Many Bambara men pray in the mosque, then visit the fetishist to get "medicine"

We've got to get back to believing that God does what He says He will do. Our church has been revolutionized. We've learned more from Africa than we've given to Africa. We've seen our people get excited about what God can do at home as well as in Africa.

to protect them from harm. Fewer (far fewer) than 1 percent of the Bambara are Christian.

They're primarily farmers living in small villages. But frequent droughts and the advance of the Sahara are steadily decreasing their food supplies. Most Bambara farmers can't produce enough food for their families year by year. Life is hard, but their eternity is hopeless without salvation through Jesus Christ. Without Jesus, an existence filled with hunger, suffering, illness, and hardship is the best they will ever experience.

But why would they listen to what we had to say about "the white man's God"?

We walked through the village that afternoon, greeted people, and went back to the mayor's "guesthouse"—a concrete floor with four walls and a roof (we actually slept outside in the dirt because it was too hot inside). After we'd eaten supper that evening, we went back down into the village. In one of the courtyards, we gathered a small crowd. By the light of a kerosene lamp, I told the story of creation. Then I told them about Jesus.

They listened politely. When I finished, I asked if there were any questions. There were several, which we answered. I said, "Well, we're staying at the mayor's guesthouse. If anyone here is interested in becoming a follower of Christ, come with us."

Ten men followed us back to the guesthouse. Steve looked at me and said, "I don't think they have a clue what they are doing. I'm going to have to explain it."

Steve spent about an hour and a half trying to "talk them out of it." By that I mean he made sure they really understood the Gospel—and

> At the end of that hour and a half, nine men prayed to receive Christ in a Muslim village where the Gospel had been proclaimed only once before.

counted the cost of a decision to follow Jesus in their culture. At the end of that hour and a half, nine men prayed to receive Christ. Remember, this was in a Muslim village where the Gospel had been proclaimed only once before, two weeks earlier, and nobody had responded.

After they made their decisions, Steve said to me, "I'm leaving the country for a while, and you're leaving here tomorrow. Nobody's going to be back out here for three or four months. We've got to teach them something." So we taught them about prayer. At about 11 or so at night, we broke out a box of Bibles and flashlights and gave a Bible to anybody who could read. By 11:30 it was about 70 degrees outside, which was freezing for them, so we said our goodbyes and prayed for them. They told us they were leaving before daylight the next day to go to market in another village, and we'd never see them again.

But when we woke up the next morning, they were standing in a circle around us, waiting for us to get up. "Please teach us again before you leave," they said. So we taught them again and left. We stopped at another Bambara village within two or three kilometers, where the chief lived. They, too, begged us to stay there and teach. In fact, the only way they would let us out of their village was if we promised to come back.

'GOD IS OUT HERE'

As soon as we got within cell-phone range of Bamako, I called missionary Marvin Thompson, who was hosting us in Mali. We were supposed to leave the next morning to visit the Soninke people, but I told Marvin, "God is out here. We need to go back to the Bambara villages."

We went back out there, and about five or six more people in the second Bambara village prayed to receive Christ. We did visit the Soninke and Bozo villages before we left Mali, but on the last night we were in the country, I sat down in a circle with the guys from my church. Everyone said the same thing: We all felt, without a shadow of a doubt, that God had called us to reach the Bambara people.

When I called Steve Roach and told him we felt led to work with him in partnership, I thought he would jump up and down for joy. But then he said, "Brad, let me tell you what that means. I want Beulah out here with a team every six weeks."

I almost choked. "Steve, we've never done this at all!" I stammered. "I was thinking once, maybe twice a year."

"That won't get it done," Steve replied. "We need you to train these new believers and start churches."

We came home and told our church what happened. I said, "We've got 15 brand-new Christians in two villages and nobody to take care of them. That would be like going to the hospital and giving birth to a baby and then just abandoning it. What are we going to do?"

Beulah folks said, "We need to go back."

Six weeks later, I got back on an airplane with another team. In three years, we've gone more than 15 times. I've lost count now, but it's been

> "We've got 15 brand-new Christians in two villages and nobody to take care of them. That would be like going to the hospital and giving birth to a baby and then just abandoning it. What are we going to do?" Beulah folks said, "We need to go back."

just about every six weeks. Sure, we've missed a couple of times; a few trips didn't quite come together. But we've kept going. We've seen God save people in "our village." We've seen the believers there take the Gospel to other villages. More than 170 new believers have come to Christ in about 20 villages. Churches have been started in six of them, and those churches are beginning to start churches.

I don't want to paint a too-rosy picture. We've encountered spiritual warfare among the Bambara. Muslims who decide to follow Christ face persecution, but it's usually social persecution. They're not threatened with death, but the Muslim leaders may say to them, "If you die, we won't bury you. We will leave your body in the fields to rot." That is a very big deal to a West African.

But word gets around about the power of Jesus Christ and how He blesses those who follow Him. Most of the Muslims in Mali are like most of the "Christians" in America. They're Muslims because they were born into Muslim families. But they want to know God. In the village where we go, the Muslim imam (mosque leader) has requested a Bible.

We've seen God save people in "our village." We've seen believers there take the Gospel to other villages. Churches have been started in six of them, and those churches are beginning to start churches. That's what it's all about.

We had a team there in 2008 and four Muslim guys came to the team's hut. They asked, "Would you pray for rain?" Our team prayed, and it began to rain immediately. The Muslims said, "We went to the imam first. He said he would pray for us but that it might take a year for God to answer his prayer. 'But the Christians are in town,' he said. 'Go to them. God always answers their prayers.'"

The new believers are having their struggles, to be sure. You read the book of Acts, and you see the internal and the external attacks the early church faced. It's the same in Mali. We've sown the seed. We've seen people come to Christ. Now they have to take the lead. Some start strong and get stronger; some don't make it. Would I make it if I were in their place? I'm not sure, to be honest.

There's no way to describe the poverty and hardship Bambara people deal with every day. We helped in 2008 with the distribution of 500 tons of grain and encountered all kinds of problems. We were well-received by the Muslims, but the Christians got mad at us. Why?

> The Muslims said, "We went to the imam first. He said he would pray for us but that it might take a year for God to answer his prayer. 'But the Christians are in town,' he said. 'Go to them. God always answers their prayers.'"

In Bambara culture, if you are responsible for a blessing that comes to your village, you're entitled to a bigger share of it. So when we came to distribute grain, the Christians said, "We're entitled to more." We told them, "No, you don't get more. You get the same amount anybody else does." They said, "The Muslims wouldn't do it that way. The Muslims wouldn't even feed us." We said, "That doesn't matter. We're doing what's right." But they went behind our backs to the chief, and they got more. That created problems for believers in other villages, and it turned into a mess.

When I got home, I wrote a letter back to the Bambara church just like the Apostle Paul would have written. I started out commending them for their faithfulness and good works, but the bottom line was: "If you guys don't repent and get this worked out, we're not coming back. We'll go to a village where they really want to obey God." Steve Roach got somebody to translate it and put it on audiotapes so the Bambara Christians could listen to it over and over again.

Well, they repented. The next time I was there, the two primary leaders looked at me and said, "Brad, when we got your letter, we remembered the story of Jesus when He said, 'Who among you, when his son asks for bread, would give him a stone, or when he asks for fish, would give him a serpent?' We know you love us, and you'd never ask us to do something that isn't right." I was overwhelmed.

There's a Bambara parable called the "Parable of the Palm Tree." The palm tree, they say, is no good because it grows tall and its leaves are thin at the top. It casts its shadow a long way from the tree and doesn't do itself any good. The meaning: Don't be like the palm tree. Take care of yourselves first before you worry about anybody else. After they repented, Steve Roach hugged all the Bambara Christians. That isn't common in their culture, so they asked, "Why are you doing this?" Steve said, "I'm just so proud that you have finally become the palm tree." They grinned and nodded their heads in understanding. Where selfishness ruled before, God overcame with love.

The next step is to get the leaders in the church there to take responsibility for bringing their own families to Christ. They have to begin to deal with what the Bible teaches about the husband being the spiritual leader in his home. What does it mean to love your wife as Christ loved the church? It's a very different culture. It's a polygamist culture. It's a culture that says it's OK to beat your wife. It's a culture that practices female circumcision. There are many difficult challenges out there.

I'm telling you, friend, it's never boring to follow God into this amazing world He has made!

WE'LL BE SOMEWHERE

At Beulah, I have been blessed of God to have people who have supported this and put their hearts into it. It has been a God thing. We don't have a budget for it. We don't pay a penny for someone to go. They have to raise their own money. The average cost for a person going on their first trip is $4,000 for a round-trip plane ticket, shots, passport, visa, and in-country costs. It's not a "cheap date" by any means.

But almost everyone who has gone with me has gone multiple times. One man in our church is 73 years old and has gone to Mali five times. His wife has gone four times. They are retired and are not wealthy, yet they have not only paid their full expenses but have paid for several other people to go. Our youngest volunteer so far, Carson Floyd, was 10 years old when he went with his parents. Two Bambara villagers asked Carson about Christ. He tried to take them to an adult volunteer, but they wanted to hear from him. So he led them to the Lord. Later he said, "That's the first two people I brought to Christ!"

> One man in our church is 73 years old and has gone to Mali five times. Our youngest volunteer so far, Carson Floyd, was 10 years old when he went with his parents.

Paul Tatton, one of our most committed volunteers, says, "I'm not going to stop coming. As long as God opens the door for me to be here, I'm gonna come."

His wife can't come, but she raises money for him. He's got a contract labor job, so he not only has to pay his way, he has to take off two weeks and not get paid. It's a very costly thing for him, but he does it joyfully.

If I had gotten up in the pulpit after that first vision trip and said, "We need to partner with IMB and go to Africa every six weeks," it probably would have been shut down before we ever got started. I just got up and said, "We've got brand-new Christians that won't get taken care of if we don't go back. What are we going to do?" We sort of grew into it.

I spoke about our experience to a group of churches considering mission partnerships. A guy raised his hand and said, "Okay, Brad, you've told us how many trips you've taken, how much money your church has spent, and none of it came out of the budget, etc. Now tell me how you did it—and don't give me the 'God' answer." I responded,

"Next question." The guy said, "Wait, you didn't answer mine!" I said, "You took away my only answer. If you take God out of the equation, there's no answer."

I tell pastors, "If God wants you to go, He's not broke. He's not in an economic crisis. If He wants you to go, He'll provide the resources." I don't know when we quit believing God does that kind of thing.

There is nothing perfect about our church—especially not the pastor. Sure, we're struggling financially like most other churches these days. The economy has continued to spiral downward. We're trimming the budget everywhere we can. But we're fighting the battle not to cut dollars from places where we see direct impact on winning people to Christ. We're doing the best we can with what God gives us.

To tell you the truth, I meet less resistance to missions from lay people than I do from other pastors. I've read that only 2.2 percent of the churches in America today are growing by reaching lost people. Do you honestly think 97.8 percent of the churches in the Southern Baptist Convention, or any other denomination, are not reaching lost people because the lay people are not willing to follow their pastor? I think we have a leadership problem. I think we as pastors quit believing God and quit challenging our people to step out in faith.

> To tell you the truth, I meet less resistance to missions from lay people than I do from other pastors. I think we have a leadership problem. I think we as pastors quit believing God and quit challenging our people to step out in faith.

Hey, I'm as guilty as everybody else. But we've got to get back to a place where we really think God does what He says He will do. As I said earlier, our church has been revolutionized. We've learned more from Africa than we've given to Africa. We experienced growth. We've seen our people get excited about what God can do at home as well as in Africa.

I'm implementing some of the strategies we use over there right here in Hopkins. The best thing I do in this church on a weekly basis is not standing in the pulpit and preaching. I love doing that, but I have a small group of men that I meet and disciple, and I think that's more significant in the long run. We're trying to get our people to step outside the culture of our church and go to work in the community where they live.

I see us always being involved in international missions. A handful of people in this church probably will always want to go to West Africa. When we finish in the Bambara village, I don't know whether God will lead us to another village there or send us to China or Mexico. I'm excited about the future. I don't know how long we'll be in Mali, but I promise you, we'll be somewhere.

After 200 years of staying home in Hopkins, we've got a lot of catching up to do.

(To see a video of members of Beulah Baptist in West Africa, go to **imb.org/beulah**.)

Chapter Six

MAKE THE CONNECTION!

We've shared how God led us to connect with His mission in our communities and around the world. What about you? Your connection journey will be unique. It won't duplicate Woodstock's path or the road taken by any other church. By far the most important part of the journey is to seek God's heart and obey His leading. He is faithful.

I've shared how God led us at Woodstock to connect with His mission in our community and around the world. Four of my brother pastors have shared how the Lord led them into a vital connection.

What about you? Do you have a burden to see your church more involved in missions? Do you want to see God use your church in supernatural ways to transform lives and communities all over the world? I believe you do—or you wouldn't be reading these words.

I want to share the following practical guide that my friends at IMB use to "coach" pastors in five key steps on the connection "journey":

1. **Awaken** to God's heart that all people may know and worship Him
2. **Explore** God's specific plan for your church
3. **Equip** your church to fulfill its mission
4. **Engage** God's specific plan for your church
5. **Multiply** your lives, mission, and ministry into other believers and churches

You may have one or more of these questions rolling around in your mind: "Where do I start? Is there someone who can sit down with me and coach me through a strategic missions process? I don't need another 'program' ... I need a relationship with people who care about my church's heart. How do I connect with opportunities, missionaries, and unreached people at home and overseas? Are resources available to help my church develop and mature its mission plan?" You will find answers to these questions in the following pages.

Your connection journey will be unique. It won't duplicate Woodstock's path or the road taken by any other church. So don't look at this simple guide as a paint-by-numbers manual. Look at it as an outline to stimulate your creative thinking and praying as you partner with Him to flesh out the exciting vision He has for your church.

By far the most important part of the journey is to seek God's heart and obey His leading. He is faithful.

I'm praying for you!

Pastor Johnny

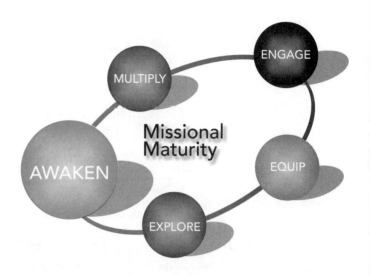

AWAKEN to God's heart that all people may know and worship Him

Awakening is a movement of God through the Holy Spirit in the hearts of church leadership and members. It cannot be manufactured or coerced but we can seek God and plead for Him to move in our hearts and the hearts of your church. 2 Chronicles 7:14

Genesis 12:1-3 The Lord said to Abram: Go out from your land, your relatives, and your father's house to the land that I will show you. I will make you into a great nation, I will bless you, I will make your name great, and you will be a blessing. I will bless those who bless you, and I will curse those who treat you with contempt, and **all the peoples on earth will be blessed through you.**

Psalms 67:1-4 May God be gracious to us and bless us; look on us with favor so that Your way may be known on earth, Your salvation **among all nations**. Let the peoples praise You, God; let all the peoples praise You. Let the nations rejoice and shout for joy, for You judge the peoples with fairness and lead the nations on earth.

2 Peter 3:9 The Lord does not delay His promise, as some understand delay, but is patient with you, **not wanting any to perish, but all to come to repentance**.

Revelation 5:9 And they sang a new song: You are worthy to take the scroll, and to open its seals; because You were slaughtered, and You redeemed [people] for God by Your blood **from every tribe and language and people and nation**.

Revelation 7:9 After this I looked, and there was a vast multitude **from every nation, tribe, people, and language**, which no one could number, standing before the throne and before the Lamb. They were robed in white with palm branches in their hands.

1 SEEK GOD'S HEART—God's desire is for you to be on mission with Him. He will provide the power, the resources, and the direction (Acts 1:8, John 15:1-11). **It starts with leadership.**

Brokenness and prayer (Isaiah 6:1-8)
» Pray that God will break hearts for His agenda.
» Pray that God will give a passion for Him to be glorified by all peoples.

Intensive Bible study (John 17:6-8)

» Search God's Word for His heart and His plan as it relates to the church and all peoples.

» Discover the theme of God's glory and reconciliation of man as a thread through the entire Bible.

True dependence on God (2 Chronicles 20:3-4; Proverbs 29:18)

» Understand that without God and His revelation, we can do nothing.

2 EMBRACE GOD'S HEART—from Genesis to Revelation, God consistently unveils His heart that some from all peoples (people groups) would personally know and worship Him.

Consider this brief synopsis of the mission thread that runs through the whole Bible

» God walked with Adam and Eve in the Garden. (Genesis 3:8)

» Abrahamic Covenant. (Genesis 12:1-3)

» God chose the people of Israel to represent Him to the nations. (Isaiah 49:6)

» Jesus became God-in-flesh to reveal the Father to us. (John 1:1-14)

» Jesus sent out the disciples to be witnesses of Him. (Acts 1:8; Matthew 28:18)

» One day people from every tribe and tongue will worship before God's throne. (Revelation 5:9)

Embrace the mission of the church

» Every believer and church has been sent to be His missionary people. (John 20:21; Acts 1:8; Matthew 28:18-19)

» Every believer and church must proclaim the Gospel. (Romans 10:11-17)

» Every believer and church represents the name of God to those who have not yet believed. (2 Corinthians 5:14-21)

Missions is not the ultimate goal of the church. Worship is. Missions exists because worship doesn't. Worship is ultimate, not missions, because God is ultimate, not man. When this age is over and the countless millions of the redeemed fall on their faces before the throne of God, missions will be no more. It is a temporary necessity. But worship abides forever.
—John Piper, *Let the Nations be Glad*

3 **SHARE GOD'S HEART**—as God awakens the hearts of leaders, there is a need for that awakening to be multiplied among the members of your church.

The message of God's heart. Because God wants all people to know and worship Him, the primary motivation behind mission is worship. Sin robs God of the glory He is due. Through God's plan of reconciliation, He made a way for His people to once again know Him and to worship Him.

God's redemptive plan is for ALL people. God has shown us in His Word that He views the world in people groups (*ta ethne*) rather than geo-political nations. Consider the Great Commission:

> *Go, therefore, and make disciples of all nations,* (panta ta ethne, Root:ethnos) *baptizing them in the name of the Father and of the Son and of the Holy Spirit.* (Matthew 28:19)

We get *ethnic* from the root ethnos. This means we must take the Gospel to every ethnic group, every tongue, every tribe, every people.

A PEOPLE GROUP is a group of individuals, frequently speaking the same language, with a shared self-identity and worldview. Strategically, a people group is the largest group through which the Gospel can flow without encountering a significant barrier.

Today there are more than 11,000 distinct people groups of which about 6,400 are considered unreached (less than 2 percent evangelical). These unreached people groups (UPG) represent 1.6 billion people and 25 percent of the world's population. Many of these people groups are not only unreached, but they also have NO access to the Gospel—meaning there is no known church, missionary, or strategy in place to reach them. These people groups are called unengaged, unreached people groups (UUPG). There are still nearly 3,500 unengaged, unreached people groups in the world.

God's method. If you have been reconciled to God and thus consider yourself a follower of Jesus Christ, then you are the tool God will use. There is no other plan. The Bible tells us that as we are reconciled to Him, we are, therefore, entrusted with the "message of reconciliation" (2 Corinthians 5:18-19). God has chosen you, the church, to be His messenger to the world. It is up to every believer and every church to proclaim the message of the Gospel to the ends of the earth. There are many who do not yet believe because they have not yet heard, and how can they hear unless you go and tell them? (Romans 10:14-15)

Ways to share God's heart

» **From the pulpit.** There is no greater point of communication in your church than the pulpit. If the cry of missions does not resonate from the heart of the pastor, impact will be limited. All other communications are simply supplemental to what comes from the heart of the pulpit. The process of instilling God's heart into the church must intentionally flow from the pulpit, but it must be real, not contrived.

» **Start with leadership.** Jesus displayed a great model for us to follow: discover and invest in faithful, available, teachable believers (2 Timothy 2:2). Church-wide awakening is more likely to happen as God works through the hearts and lives of the church's leadership (pastors, elders, staff, deacons, ministry leaders, mission team, teachers, etc.).

God wants to be worshipped and to receive glory
from all people groups.
He has chosen to use you, His church, to be His ambassador.
How will God use your church in His plan?
What unreached peoples will He lead you to disciple?
Through what relationships can you begin to
disciple unreached peoples?

Utilize intentional Bible studies

» **Church-wide small group focus.** There are several options for six- to eight-week Bible studies that could be used in small group or Sunday School ministries.

- » **Discipleship class.** Many churches offer ongoing discipleship studies in addition to their Sunday School or small group ministry.
- » **Church-wide study** can involve both small group study and a concurrent sermon series.

Focused prayer strategy. Develop an intentional prayer time during small groups and worship services to pray that God will begin to break hearts and to instill His heart in the church. For even greater emphasis, consider intentional prayer times other than regularly scheduled services.

Missionary guests. As available, invite missionaries to share field experiences and opportunities. This can be done in person or via Internet video links during a church service.

Printed/visual media. Be creative. Many free and low-cost resources are available at imb.org.

Discover and utilize all existing and available communication media—bulletin inserts, newsletters, small group announcements, e-mails, videos, posters, etc.

Consider developing a mission area. Pick a focal spot in the church facility and use resources such as maps, magazines, photos, videos, stories, displays, etc.

Personal interaction. As you and others are awakened by God's call to missions, you should pray for and share with those who have not yet experienced this passion.

EXPLORE God's specific plan for your church

If God wants to be worshipped by all people groups and He has chosen the church to be His messenger, how does He want you, the church, to partner with Him in His plan? Who does He want you to reach, where will you reach them and with whom does He want you to partner in order to reach them?

1 **ASSEMBLE A TEAM**—Involvement is crucial to mobilizing the whole church in the mission. Allowing others to be involved in the exploring process will create and invite ownership, which will in turn lead to even more involvement.

Identify existing leaders with a missions passion—mission team/committee, project leaders, staff, lay leaders, etc.

Select team members based on spiritual health and skill set. As exploring for God's will is a spiritual exercise, it is more important to select team members who have an intimate walk with God than people who have simply been active in missions. It is also important to remember that some people are fulfilled by doing, not by developing strategy. If you put "doers" on this exploration team, they may be frustrated. Placing the right individuals on the team in the correct roles will greatly impact the outcome of the process.

Consider developing a temporary exploration team. If you do not have a currently active and functioning mission team, it may be good to form a temporary team that will help develop a preliminary mission strategy for your church. This will give time to observe and identify those individuals best suited to serve on the team long term.

2 DEVELOP MISSIONAL VALUES—There will be many opportunities to become involved in missions. To prevent unfocused, ineffective activity, develop values that will guide ongoing involvement and strategy.

Start with a biblical end vision
- » Strive for a comprehensive plan remembering that God wants ALL people groups to know and worship Him. (Revelation 5:9; 7:9)
- » Plan to engage the least reached or unreached peoples both locally and globally. (Acts 1:8)
- » Plan for long-term commitment. Because discipleship is the goal, not just conversion. Therefore long-term involvement is essential. (Matthew 28:18-19)

» Understand that the local church is God's plan for ongoing disciple making. Therefore, church planting among ALL people groups is a must.

Establish a foundational strategy

» Seek God for His specific direction.

» Understanding the end vision develops the process steps or activities that will be appropriate.

» Begin to identify the personality and skill set of the church.

EXAMPLE OF A FOUNDATIONAL MISSION STRATEGY

Community Transformation

Establish Churches

- Develop relationships
- Share the Gospel
- Identify and develop leaders
- Gather the believers
- Multiply

Be a Blessing

- Assess needs
- Develop processes for meeting needs
- Invest in long-term solutions

PRAYER

3 IDENTIFY YOUR EXISTING RELATIONSHIPS

Has God already sent people out from your church to the mission field? The biblical model is that God calls out people from your church, and the church responds obediently by sending them. Sending depicts partnering. As God calls people out of your church, they are not disconnecting from your church but rather are sent out as representatives from the local church. There is a genuine responsibility of the "sender" to partner with the "sent" and a responsibility of the "sent" to be accountable to the "senders."

As Southern Baptists, we already have relationships that can become partnerships. IMB, North American Mission Board, your state convention, and your local association are ready and eager to help you develop new or strengthen existing relationships.

Are there existing relationships already that fit in your missional values?

» Missionaries who have been sent from your church?
» Missionaries who have visited your church or with whom you may have worked in the past?
» Church planters either sent from or to your area?

4 IDENTIFY UNREACHED PEOPLES

People group definition. A people group is a group of individuals, frequently speaking the same language, with a shared self-identity and worldview. Strategically, a people group is the largest group through which the Gospel can flow without encountering a significant barrier.

» Identifying unreached people groups will require an intentional and careful look at your own community, nation, and the least reached parts of the world. Understand that disciple making takes time, energy, and love. Identify people groups with a plan to minister long term until they have experienced life and community transformation.

But you will receive power when the Holy Spirit comes on you; and you will be my witnesses in Jerusalem, and in all Judea and Samaria, and to the ends of the earth. (Acts 1:8)

Possible discovery questions

» What are the current mission activities/partnerships of your church and how effective are these activities as they relate to discipling unreached peoples and the missional values?

» Within current relationships, are there any unreached peoples you can adopt?

» Are there unreached people groups on the heart of the pastor or the hearts of key leaders in the church?

» Are there pockets of lostness in the church community that are not currently being effectively engaged with the Gospel (i.e., students, cowboys, affinity groups, ethnic groups, geographical area, etc.)?

Possible discovery methods

» **Websites:** peoplegroups.org || peoplegroups.info || joshuaproject.net

» **Contact** local social, government, health, and school officials.

» **Counsel** with your IMB missional church strategist for additional helps and resources. To find your strategist, go to imb.org, click on Lead your church, then Who we are. Click on your state for the contact information of your mobilization strategist and give him a call!

» **Demographic studies:** Go to namb.net, click on Mission Resources, then Missional Research, then Knowing Community, then Demographic Reports.

» **Global Research:** imb.org/globalresearch

» **State partnerships:** sbc.net/stateconvassoc.asp

Developing a Comprehensive Acts 1:8 Strategy

Crossing geographical and cultural barriers to take the Gospel to all peoples

	Closest to the Gospel **Reached**	**Access**	**Unreached**	Farthest from the Gospel **Unengaged**
Nearest to you	Who, How, With Whom:	Who, How, With Whom:	Who, How, With Whom:	Who, How, With Whom:
Farthest from you				

Geographic determination based on proximity

© imb 2009

5 CHOOSE A FOCUS PEOPLE GROUP

Study your unreached peoples. As people groups are identified, begin to study, know, and love them.

» Study their culture.
  • Primary language
  • Primary religion(s)
  • Discover cultural landmines that may prevent long-term effectiveness (i.e., clothing, touching with your left hand, showing bottoms of shoes, etc.).
  • Identify barriers to understanding the Gospel.
  • Discover where they live worldwide (locally and globally).

God has a specific plan for your church to engage unreached peoples both locally and globally. How can you equip your church to be effectively engaged in what God has called you to do?

» Seek possible relational bridges that can be built.
  • What special skills or knowledge does the church offer that may be beneficial to your people group (i.e., medical, education, agriculture, trades, business, training, etc.)?
  • Consider holistic ministry, meeting physical, emotional, and spiritual needs. (1 Thessalonians 5:23)
  • Develop relationships, become friends.
  • Pray that God will increase your burden and love for these people.

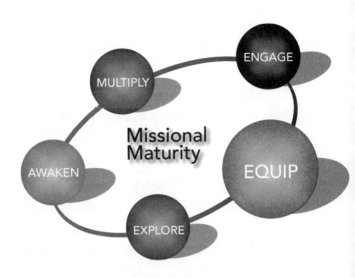

EQUIP the church to fulfill the mission

1 EDUCATE YOUR CHURCH FOR THE MISSION

Develop an overall mission education process that crosses all age and/or affinity groups in your church.

Include the whole church. Look for ways to educate the entire body, including those who do not attend small groups.

Penetrate all ministry areas of the church. Since missions is the mission of the church, all departments/areas of ministry must be included: students, men, women, worship, children, education, etc. Develop creative ways for every segment of the church to be involved at some level.

2 EDUCATE YOUR CHURCH WITH THE VISION

What is the end vision? What is your church striving to accomplish in penetrating lostness and your unreached people groups?

Communicate a clear definition of the mission.

Communicate the scope and length of commitments.

» Will you adopt missionaries or unreached peoples for a specific time period?

» Will you adopt missionaries or unreached peoples until specific goals are accomplished?

Develop an ongoing communication process to inspire the church body to understand the vision and grow in love of identified unreached peoples.

Clearly communicate what you want church members to do. What are your church's members expected to do as it relates to the mission strategy and reaching the unreached?

Adoption principle: for long-term impact and missional effectiveness, identify and adopt unreached people groups until they are able to reach and disciple their own people and begin to move toward cross-cultural missions themselves.

3 EQUIP YOUR CHURCH FOR THE MISSION

Increase cultural understanding. Equip your church to understand their personal worldview and how it compares to the worldview of the identified unreached peoples. Remember that the Gospel flows within the medium of culture.

» What are distinguishing characteristics of the identified peoples?

» What is their primary language?

» What are some cultural landmines that could prevent long-term effectiveness?

» What are the barriers that may keep your adopted people group from hearing and receiving the Gospel?

Teach and embrace biblical, practical, and reproducible missiology. Use discernment as you work to understand possible cultural implications of your actions.

» **Beware of dependency.** While striving to make disciples, be careful to use resources and methods that your unreached peoples can ultimately model and reproduce themselves. Do not create an environment where outside resources are necessary to perpetuate the disciple-making process.

» **Guard against syncretism.** In many cultures, it is easy for the unreached peoples to simply "add" Jesus to the existing primary religion to which they already adhere. In the Hindu religion, there are more than 300 million gods, it would be very natural for them to add Jesus as "one" of their gods. Be committed to stress and preach the message that faith in Jesus Christ ALONE is the ONLY way to salvation and right relationship with the Father. Be sure to emphasize repentance from sin and false religion. (John 14:6)

» **Learn to contextualize the Gospel.** The message of the Gospel NEVER changes, but the methods used to communicate the Gospel must adjust so the people can understand it within their own culture (heart language). The goal of missions strategy is not to work against existing culture in order to implant new culture. The goal is to understand and work within existing culture to share the Gospel in a way it can be understood and then disseminated to others within that culture. Allow the adopted peoples to worship in their context while at the same time adhering to biblical doctrine. (example: Mars Hill, Acts 17:16-34)

Uphold the basic unchanging principles of missions

» The ONLY hope for mankind is Jesus Christ! He is the only way of salvation. Truly, all the church has to offer the lost of the world is the message of hope in Jesus Christ.

» God wants to be known among ALL people. Realizing and embracing this concept leads His followers out of their comfort zones to reach those who are different from them.

» God desires and commands all of His children, Christians, to partner with Him in His mission. As part of the body of Christ, every authentic Christian must play his or her part in His plan. The overall goal of a church is to mobilize every part of the body of Christ to play its part in discipling the unreached peoples—whether it be through fervent prayer, sacrificial giving, going to proclaim, or sending others.

Embrace flexibility for the sake of communicating the Gospel through the medium of your adopted unreached people's culture. On the mission field, there are times when long-range planning has to change—sometimes daily!

» Be committed to the end vision but stay flexible in methodology.

» Be willing to die to personal culture so that disciples can be made.

» Learn to love the adopted peoples unconditionally.

Develop an ongoing training process for team leaders and team members.

» Team member training, team leader training, and more are tools that are available through IMB resources (imbresources.org). IMB believes it is essential for you to include Safe Travel Solutions in your equipping process. (safetravelsolutions.org).

Organize for effectiveness. IMB highly recommends that your pastor/mission leader register your church to utilize the Web-based mission tool called imbCONNECT.net. The leader signs up to obtain the credentials and password necessary to use the tool. Then the pastor/mission leader will invite all other team members into your church's private mission site. To obtain your credentials and password, go to imbCONNECT.net. Coaching to use this tool is available from your missional church strategist at IMB or call the church mobilization specialist assigned to your state at (800) 999-3113. This tool is useful for all local and global mission planning.

4 ORGANIZE YOUR CHURCH TO FULFILL THE MISSION

Develop teams that will move your church to be more effective in the missions strategy. Possible teams could include:

» **Acts 1:8 team.** Oversee and develop ongoing strategy, create necessary policies and procedures, and seek ongoing partnership opportunities. Possible team goals:
  • Define partnership levels
  • Define your missions policies
  • Set parameters for new partnerships
  • Create budgeting and funding processes

- Set policies for short-term trips, fund raising, new ideas, team leading, etc.
- Create a sending process—be prepared for those God calls out for lifetime, cross-cultural work.
- Develop and evaluate engagement strategies
- Oversee ongoing church-wide mobilization process

» **Communication team.** Develop ongoing processes for utilizing available media or creating new media to continually update the church about your partnerships. This would include stories and/or needs from the field, service opportunities, missions understanding, etc.

» **Prayer team.** Develop ongoing processes to help mobilize your church to pray consistently, specifically, and fervently.

Identify and train leaders.

Identify individuals with specific skills the people of your church possess.

Remember, involvement leads to ownership. As more and more people are invited to be a part of the missions strategy, ownership, in most cases, will increase exponentially. As needs arise, allow for more opportunities for more people to be involved at many different levels.

ENGAGE in God's specific plan for your church

1 LEARN EXISTING STRATEGY

Realize and support existing, effective field strategy.

Learn from those with greater cultural understanding.

When possible, work with—not in spite of—existing workers.

Find ways to strengthen strategy.

2 GO TO THE UNREACHED PEOPLES—to carry out what God has called the church to do.

Discovery trips. Send groups to where the adopted peoples are located, whether locally or globally. Seek to:

» Learn culture

» Discover potential partners

» Identify needs

» Search for potential opportunities to engage

» Seek the persons of peace.

Short-term teams. In fulfillment of the end vision and mission strategy, send trained and prepared teams regularly, consistently and often so trust can be earned and the adopted peoples may be discipled. Possible activities could include:

» Prayerwalking

» Evangelism

» Social ministry

» Local schools

» Skills training

» Leadership development

» Bridge building—sport camps, medical clinics, English classes, business training, etc.

Long-term

» Your church may, in many cases, be "the missionary."

» Be prepared for the real possibility that a team member may feel called to a longer involvement, i.e., six months, a year, or more.

» Pray for and expect God to call some for life-time, cross-cultural missions.

Do whatever it takes

» Pray for God to identify ways to facilitate genuine life and community transformation.

» Be willing to take risks.

» Commit time and resources until the adopted peoples are reached and discipled.

» Serve with passion, persistence, and tenacity.

» Sacrifice comfort and desires.

» Seek to involve other churches, individuals and/or organizations.

3 EVALUATE THE PROGRESS

» Compare progress as it relates to the end vision.

» Commit to function, not form.

» Be fluid, ready to respond to needed changes.

» Be flexible when on the mission field.

» Be sensitive to the Holy Spirit's leading.

» Seek to strengthen or modify relationships for the sake of greater effectiveness.

» Develop an ongoing evaluation process to compare current activity to the overall end vision.

MULTIPLY your lives, mission, and ministry into other believers

1 FOLLOW THE BIBLICAL MODELS OF MULTI-PLICATION

Multiplication of churches—the model demonstrated in the book of Acts.

- » Acts 1:15—church is recorded having 120 souls.
- » Acts 2:41—3,000 added.
- » Acts 2:47—the Lord added day by day.
- » Acts 4:4—5,000 men added.
- » Acts 5:14—multitudes of men and women added.
- » Acts 6:7—number of disciples "multiplied greatly."
- » Acts 9:31—now numbering "churches," not individuals.
- » Acts 11:21—"great number."

» Acts 16:5—the mission turned into a church-planting movement.

Multiplication into the life of other believers. 2 Timothy 2:2 "And what you have heard from me in the presence of many witnesses, commit to faithful men who will be able to teach others also."

Before anything else can happen, we must dedicate effort into prayer, asking God to move the hearts of people and churches for the mission. We can exhort, equip, and encourage, but only God can move the heart of believers into the harvest. Dedicate seasons of prayer at appropriate times in the life of your church to ask God to call out those individuals specially chosen for the mission. Matthew 9:37-38

2 ENLIST—THOSE TO DISCIPLE AND MENTOR

Pray

» Pray for members
» Pray for church leaders
» Pray for other pastors and churches

Actively invite

Only God can change hearts, but it is incumbent on us to ask and provide opportunities for other churches to respond and enlist in service to the King in His mission.

Relationships are essential. Identify other churches, pastors, and missions leaders with whom you have an existing relationship. Actively invite them to join you in the mission. Seek ways to mentor them in a missional growth journey.

Use special missions presentations, impact weekends, and celebrations to invite those you want to partner with and mentor. Consider never going on a mission trip as a church without including at least one pastor and lay leader from another church.

3 EQUIP

Give—as a way of encouragement, give a partial scholarship to someone who has never been on a strategic mission trip before.

Go with those you enlist so they, too, can experience, taste, and feel missions.

Guide them through their own journey of awakening, exploring, equipping, engaging, and multiplying in missions involvement.

Model servant leadership—don't walk with them as a superior but as a fellow pilgrim on the journey.

Be like Paul—"Be imitators of me, as I also am of Christ." (1 Corinthians 11:1).

4 ENCOURAGE

  » Be mutually accountable
  » Meet together regularly
  » Pray together
  » Be available

CONNECTION POINTS

Ready to connect to God's global mission? Let us help you plug in on the greatest adventure your church will ever experience. Here are key "connection points" where you can find personal encouragement, additional information, and ideas to help you get started.

Find connection points and helpful resources
from IMB, First Baptist Woodstock, Johnny Hunt, Timothy+Barnabas, and Global Focus at:

getconnectedglobally.com

Or call or e-mail:
IMB
(800) 999-3113, option 3 • imb@imb.org

FIRST BAPTIST WOODSTOCK
(770) 926-4428 • themission@fbcw.net

GLOBAL FOCUS
(770) 529-8610 • jim.sheffield@globalfocus.info

If you have a QR reader on your mobile phone, scan this code to go to *getconnectedglobally.com*. Standard data rates may apply.